EVERY DAY I'M
HUSTLING

EVERY DAY I'M HUSTLING

VIVICA A. FOX

WITH KEVIN CARR O'LEARY

ST. MARTIN'S PRESS ☙ NEW YORK

EVERY DAY I'M HUSTLING. Copyright © 2018 by Vivica A. Fox. All rights reserved. Printed in the United States of America. For information, address St. Martin's Press, 175 Fifth Avenue, New York, N.Y. 10010.

www.stmartins.com

Endpaper photograph © Blake Little Photography

The Library of Congress Cataloging-in-Publication Data is available upon request.

ISBN 978-1-250-13445-5 (hardcover)
ISBN 978-1-250-13446-2 (ebook)
ISBN 978-1-250-19890-7 (signed edition)

Our books may be purchased in bulk for promotional, educational, or business use. Please contact your local bookseller or the Macmillan Corporate and Premium Sales Department at 1-800-221-7945, extension 5442, or by email at MacmillanSpecialMarkets@macmillan.com.

First Edition: April 2018

10 9 8 7 6 5 4 3 2 1

This book is dedicated to the memory of my late father, William E. Fox.

CONTENTS

Part Four: Look Amazing at Any Age or Budget

Part Five: Maintaining Success as You Grow Through Change

PREFACE

I don't know what brought you to this book, darling, but I am so glad you're here.

Maybe you got knocked down and you need a little help getting back up. Perhaps you invested in loving the wrong person. Maybe you don't even know where to start on your dream and you see everyone else in this Instagram-filtered world living theirs. I've been there.

Let me tell you a secret. When I was a little girl growing up in Indianapolis, no one could say "Vivica." I used to get called "Vuh-vee-sha" or "Vi-vike-a," anything but the right way. And, honestly, most folks just couldn't be bothered. I was so sensitive about my name that I made it easy for everyone else, going by a shortening of my middle name, Anjanetta. "You can call me Angie," I'd say, like an apology. In life sometimes we run away from the things that make us unique.

I didn't become Vivica until I came to California and met my first casting director at an audition. I told her my real name, then quickly blurted out my usual, "But it's okay, you can call me Angie."

"Why? You have a beautiful name," she said. "As a matter of fact you should be Vivica A. Fox, so people will always remember you as 'Vivica's a fox.'"

And honey, I thought I was gold. By 1992, I'd been on an episode of *The Fresh Prince of Bel-Air* and landed a spot on an NBC sitcom by the same creator. The show was called *Out All Night*, and I got to play the daughter of none other than Miss Patti LaBelle. *Out All Night* was set in a club, so I was meeting musical guests like Luther Vandross, Mary J. Blige, TLC, and Mark Wahlberg when he was just Marky Mark. I made the cover of *Jet*, and I knew those people back home in Indianapolis could say my name now. I had made it.

Then one morning we all came in for a table read. We'd taped a show the night before, and I thought we killed it. "Yeah, you killed it," someone said. "The show's canceled. Clean out your shit."

They weren't even going to air the last show. Now, I wish I had a tape of myself crying at that table, because, Lord, it would show how deep and ugly I can go as an actress. I was in such a state that Miss Patti couldn't believe it. "Child, you crying so much you 'bout to turn white," she joked. "You're gonna be all right. You'll see."

Here I had one of the most talented and experienced entertainers in history telling me I would be okay, but I couldn't hear it. I was devastated. I was living in this cute little condo in Inglewood, thinking I'd made it. I'd put two thousand miles between little Angie and the person I wanted to be. And now I was losing it all.

It got worse. I would go on audition after audition, watching my bank account dwindle as each time I would make it to the final callback . . . and then they'd go with the bigger-named black actress. At the time, Jasmine Guy from *A Different World* was the "It" girl blowing up. Me, I was just blown up.

Finally, I had to call home to tell my mom I was in trouble. Everlyena Fox spent my childhood working. She was a single mom who held down two jobs to provide for us four kids after my parents divorced when I was four. She believed in two things: work and God.

I'll never forget the call. I gingerly told her I might need a bit of a loan. "If you can help me out . . ." She said yes, and I cried. And I told her, "Okay, I'm not going to be calling and asking for money again, so I've got to figure this shit out."

"Write a letter," Mom told me. "Put it in your Bible and pray about it. *He will bring it back to you.*"

So I got on my knees. And I wrote this:

I want to be successful. I want to be a star and I want to work as an actress. And I've got a taste of things, but it seems I can't get over the hump. It seems I'm always almost just making it and then coming up a little bit short.

If you could just help me to stay focused and help me to stay positive, I promise that I'll be good. And do good. And give back.

Maybe you're feeling the same way. You just can't get over that hump and you keep coming up a little bit short. For me, the answer came when I asked. And the answer was to get to work.

And keep at it. I worked my ass off—sometimes literally—to get *Independence Day*, *Set It Off*, and *Kill Bill*. I took risks to get *Curb Your Enthusiasm* and was offered the role on *Empire* because Lee Daniels liked how I handled myself with the silliness on *Celebrity Apprentice*. I got to return to the big screen as Jasmine in *Independence Day: Resurgence* and be the Head Chick in Charge on my own show, *Vivica's Black Magic*. My grind don't stop, and people notice.

Sure, there've been failures and heartbreak in relationships. I'm working on that, trust and believe. You can also trust that as a single black actress in my fifties, I understand struggle. I get up every day to fight for my place in Hollywood. And sometimes I'm still my own worst critic, looking at what's wrong instead of what's right. Just this week I saw a paparazzi photo of me walking out of something with my arm waving. *See, you had your arm up and look at that tummy*, I said to myself. *You look a little fat through there.*

And then I had to say, *Snap out of it, bitch. You gotta be your biggest cheerleader. Get out of your own way.*

I want to help you as you get out of your own way, too. Now, my language can be what I call "street but sweet"—my friends didn't nickname me Ghetto Barbie for nothing. But I can also take you to church. The Lord loves a scrappy girl.

I owe this book to my mother, who told me to write down *my* dream. But this book is not about making a wish. I want to provide concrete, real strategies for realizing—or even just figuring out— *your* dream.

And I hope it's a big one. There's nothing wrong with having big dreams. It just means you have to put in more effort. Some people today think they can swipe right or press send and something can happen overnight, and you don't have to work for nothing. It's so different from what I know to be the truth. I have had to work for every damn thing. My mama told me growing up, "You're gonna work. I don't care if you think you're cute. Yes, you are, but your ass is gonna work."

So take my hand, darling, and let's work together.

PART ONE

THE
START
OF OUR
HUSTLE

IF YOU HANG WITH THE BIG BOYS, YOU'RE GONNA GET KNOCKED DOWN

wanted to look like a goddess.

This spring the beauty magazine *Sheen* threw me a party naming me Woman of the Year, so I felt I had to look the part. They had flown me from L.A. and put me up in a lovely suite in the Atlanta Marriott Marquis. I still had a few minutes before I needed to head downstairs to the black-tie gala, so I did one last check in the full-length mirror.

My hair was up high and off my face, and my makeup artist Daryon Haylock had given me a smoky eye, glowy skin, and a bold lip. For a big event we always put just a little glitter on my face, a little shimmer to feel regal.

Instead of an LBD, I went with a little black Alexander McQueen gown that my girl at Neiman Marcus Beverly Hills, Bani, helped me pick out. A halter-neck, down-to-the-ground stretch-knit, the dress hugged every curve and accented all of my assets. The dress showed off my arms—which you know I had been putting some extra work into defining since I picked the gown—and it had a tasteful cutout to show the cleavage. The girls were sittin' up proper, I thought, running my fingers over the dress's jeweled neckline. This wide collar of sparkling jewels was what sold me on the dress. It reminded me of Audrey Hepburn's diamond necklace in *Breakfast at Tiffany's*.

"Woman of the Year," I whispered to myself, turning to get the whole look. Usually at this age Hollywood tells women they're going to put you out to pasture. Actually, they don't really tell you—they just make you invisible. If you don't get the hint and go quietly, they will knock you down. Time and again, I have done myself the favor of getting back up.

There was a knock at my hotel room door. It was my big brother Marvin with his wife, Thelma, and their eight-year-old son, Myles Ryan. They live near Atlanta, and one of the reasons I was so excited about the gala was that I could share the night with them.

"Looking good, sister-in-law," Thelma said as I hugged Marvin.

"Right back at'cha, sister-in-law," I said.

Myles Ryan was so cute in his gray suit vest and blue-striped tie. "You ready to do this?" I asked.

My little nephew broke into his megawatt smile. "Yes, Sparkle T.T.," he said. He has always called me that, starting when he was a little baby who couldn't take his eyes off my diamond earrings. I'd kiss his cute face, and he would reach for them and say, "Sparkle."

When we got downstairs, photographers waited at the entrance to the party. I was posing up, really giving a "She has arrived!" performance, and then I started laughing. I noticed Marvin and his family were standing off to the side, not sure what to do.

"Come here," I said, waving them in to stand beside me. "This is about you, too. I wouldn't be here without you, Brotha Marv."

Flashbulbs went off on the four of us, and I drew Myles Ryan closer to me. There was not an ounce of nerves to this beautiful child, and his megawatt smile shone even brighter in the cameras' flash. He loved the attention.

"Look at you," I told him. "You're a star."

Myles looked up at me and got this little glint in his eye that reminded me so much of pictures of me as a kid.

"That's right," I said, assuring him the same way I would tell myself when I was a kid. "We are stars."

Let me tell you a story from back in the day.

I was six years old, two years out from my parents' divorce. My dad was visiting my mom's home in Indianapolis, and we four kids were all with him in the backyard. My mama had a cute little green house, wood-framed and about a thousand square feet of us kids crowding each other. We were two blocks from the projects, nestled in a long row of ranch houses with just-washed cars parked on concrete driveways.

Everlyena Fox had worked two jobs to buy her own home and live a life of independence. My mother had grown up a West Point, Mississippi, farm girl, used to working from sunup to sundown. Her childhood was all about milking cows, shooing pigs, and picking cotton. School was her salvation. She walked the miles back and forth from school like it was a higher calling, and graduated from West Point High School.

I once asked what parts of farm living she enjoyed. She laughed.

"Nothing," she said.

On her own with four kids at thirty-two, my mom brought that same dedication to providing for us. And to proving that she would never, ever have to rely on anyone for a single thing again. Especially my father. William Fox was that city boy who got him a good old country girl and brought her up to Indy. They met when she was twenty-one, while she was visiting her older brother in Elkhart, Indiana.

"She had an extreme beauty and poise," my father, who was eighty at the time, told me, remembering when he and my mother were young. "She was like a Sophia Loren. And I wooed her with my city swag."

And he broke her heart. I'm a daddy's girl to this day, don't get me wrong, but I know he broke her heart.

So whenever Dad visited, my mother made herself scarce, which wasn't hard for her to do when she was working so damn much. Breakups are never easy, as I've learned.

It was summer, and my big brothers, Marvin and Sandy, were playing basketball at the hoop my dad had set up for them. Marvin, our family's quiet go-getter, was ten. Sandy, the most athletic and mellow of our family, was seven. Our big sister, Sugie, already our Mama Bear at eleven, was left to play mother while our mom worked. That day she was fussing over me, telling me not to run around quite so much or I might get hurt. Marvin's nickname for me was Cartwheel Angie, because I was always spinning, running, having fun. My mother used to say, "Now, that one there of mine, oh, she's busy. She *always* busy." My mother has a Southern voice that flows slow like honey, and I can hear her telling me, exasperated, "Sit your little hyper self there."

Dad was shouting pointers at Marvin and Sandy as I watched them fly around the backyard with the ball. Any time spent with my dad revolved around sports, and back then my brothers always got the lion's share of his time and attention. He'd take them to wrestling matches and Indiana Pacers games at the State Fairgrounds, and the boys would come home thrilled, so pepped up from what they'd seen.

I wanted in.

So I jumped for the ball, yelling, "I want to play, I want to play!"

Now, I was a bitty thing, no bigger than a minute, but man, did I take that ball. I was perfection on that court for three, maybe four seconds.

And then Sandy, quiet sweet Sandy, knocked me right over with one jab. I was embarrassed and mad. I ran over to my father, reaching out my arms to be held, a flood of tears about to roll down my cheeks.

"Unh-unh," Dad said. "Ain't no crying. Can't be doing that."

Hold up. I was the baby of the family—didn't everyone have to be sweet to me?

Then he told me something that's carried me through these five decades. "Angie, if you want to hang with the big boys, you're gonna get knocked down. *It's on you to get up.*"

You're going to get knocked down. And it is on you to get up.

It's a lesson you might not see in most self-help or business books, so let me be the one to tell you: Success does not guarantee the absence of getting your ass kicked.

The next time I went in to play with my brothers, damn straight they knocked me down. But I got up. Playing with the big boys made me a better player. And I kept playing with them until I could beat them fair.

Dad started taking me along to Pacers games, and he played basketball with me when he visited. He worked with me on my jump shot until I could nail it and do the Fox family proud. I also got to tag along with my brothers to the Coliseum to see wrestling matches. This was the WWA, an Indianapolis-based early version of the WWF. No frills but plenty of drama. Our favorite was Dick the Bruiser, a bald-headed monster who took on some cocky up-and-comer every week. He'd demolish the new guy as we cheered.

I was trying to fit in so much with my brothers that they taught me all the wrestling moves, from the backbreaker to the headlock.

I got put in so many choke holds. If I was cute with them, I got punished. I think that's what made me so tough.

As I was growing into a jock like my brothers, it made me very different from my big sister, Sugie. My sister will tell it to you like it is, but she's always had such a sweetness to her that no one called her by her real name, Alecia. It was "Shhhuuuugie," drawn out like that feeling of eating a piece of pie after a religious fast—or a juice cleanse, whatever you believe in.

Mom made it clear Sug was in charge, and I think that was hard on her as a kid. I know she was proud that my mother felt she could trust her. But Sug had to alternate between being a little mama telling us what to do and a regular teenager who was discovering boys. The Foxes had a reputation for being good-looking, and I thought she was the most beautiful girl in the world. As I followed her lead in all things, she taught me how to be cool. She was popular, and because she was stuck watching me, she would let me tag along with her friends.

One Friday night I went along with her to USA East, the big roller-skating rink in Indianapolis. "We're gonna teach you how to skate," she told me. USA East was a wonderland on Friday nights, the lights down low with spotlights of color dotting the floor. I was there with all these big kids roller-dancing with their hands in the air to great music like Stevie Wonder's "Signed, Sealed, Delivered." I wanted so bad to be as good as her out there, but I wiped out again and again.

"I keep falling," I said to her the umpteenth time I landed on my ass.

"Falling is part of it, Angie," she said. "You'll get it."

Now I hear the echo of what my dad taught me about getting back up. Sug was just as much an influence on me. We shared a bedroom and the boys had their room. I let Sug have the big closet and I took the little one. I always gave way for Sug, especially once she got a job. She started working at Target and needed to dress on point. But, oh, I always stole her clothes. She hated that. I was in such a rush to grow up that I didn't care if I drowned in them. I was a good sneak, but one time I let my friend Sheila Bee borrow one of Sug's cowl-neck sweaters, back when cowl-necks were really in. "She ain't gonna know," Sheila told me. Then her fool ass got makeup on the collar. Sugie knew all right, and beat my butt but good.

Sugie cooked for us, all the things that Mama taught her, and she always stretched the meal with tons of rice. She also made hot-water cornbread exactly to my mama's Mississippi standards. Now, I'm not what I call a "cooker," but I saw Sugie and Mama make it enough times to tell you how.

SUG'S HOT-WATER CORNBREAD

Now, all families are different. This is how Sug does it. Some people like them a bit sweeter and they put in sugar. Sug is sweet enough.

- 1½ cups Aunt Jemima Self-Rising White Corn Meal*
- 1 egg
- About ⅔ cup of boiling, scalding, super hot water
- Grease or lard—you could also use leftover bacon fat

Get that grease or lard nice and hot in the pan. Use enough.

Meanwhile, mix the corn meal in a bowl with the egg. Slowly add the hot water, stirring with the back of a fork until it's cakey like Play-Doh. If it's too loose and mushy, you put in

* Okay, there are areas that are deprived of self-rising corn meal in grocery stores. Amazon will hook you up! Order it Prime and rush it over.

too much water. Just add more corn meal. Too dry, add more water.

Spoon or pour desired amount pancake-style into the hot grease or lard. Flip them when you see the edges begin to brown. When both sides are golden brown, you're done.

The cornbread is so nice on a plate of black-eyed peas, which Sug always cooks up on New Year's Day. It's a traditional food that welcomes a prosperous new year. Here's how she does it:

SUG'S CROCK-POT BLACK-EYED PEAS

First things first: Soak the beans overnight. It's worth it. Nobody suddenly says, "I'm going to make black-eyed peas this instant." No, you plan for it. It's an event.

- 16-ounce bag of dry black-eyed peas (soaked overnight)
- 1 pound of meat (salt pork, smoked ham shank, smoked turkey wing, turkey leg, etc.)
- 1 small onion, diced
- Water
- Lawry's Seasoned Salt to taste

Before you soak the beans, do a quick sort-through to make sure there are no little stones or rotten beans. Soak the beans overnight, leaving a few inches of water covering them. Once the beans have soaked, drain and rinse them.

Place the meat in the Crock-Pot, then add in the beans and diced onion. Pour in enough water to cover everything. Liberally salt with Lawry's.

Set the Crock-Pot to low for about 4 hours. Taste and add more Lawry's if needed. Discard the bones and break up the meat. Serve and welcome abundance.

As you welcome abundance with gratitude, know that I am so grateful for the blessing that is my sister. I adore Sug. She loves with all of her heart. Every single time I play a mother, whether I'm in the kitchen in *Soul Food* or running through the desert in *Independence Day*, you can see some Sug up on that screen. I even had a big roller-skating scene in *Soul Food* during a flashback. And yes, that was me falling on cue. More than that, in *Soul Food*, I used the way she talks to her beautiful daughter, Sharday, to capture that mix of love, concern, and bemusement when I had to sweetly keep my on-screen son in line. In fact, after she saw it, Sug called me.

"Angie, you were playing me in that movie, weren't you?"

"Yes, I was, Sugie." I wasn't sure how she would take it. "You inspired me because you have always been the glue that holds the family together."

"Well, you did a good job," she said. "You skated real nice, too."

That meant the world to me. Growing up, Sugie definitely became my surrogate mom. She provided structure and accountability in a house that could have gone kind of wild if she had shrunk from the responsibility of caring for us. When we speak as adults, I can give her all the gratitude I have. But back then I took her for granted. At a young age, she was not asked to be our shadow parent. It was *assumed* she would step in. Sug had to not only demonstrate maturity to us, her three siblings, but also be an example of leadership in the absence of parents. Through her day-to-day actions, she taught me that you can say "family comes first" all you want, but you have to do the work to back it up. She's still doing it to this day, keeping all of us "kids" tied together no matter where we go in the world. And now she and her daughter have the close relationship I wish that my mother and me could have.

A little while ago, a camera crew went with me back to Indy, wanting to see where I grew up. I took them to see my mom, who still lives in my childhood home. And this rude woman from the crew straight up said, "Why do you have your mother still living in such a little house?"

She doesn't know Everlyena Fox. Here's the answer every time I ask my mom if she'd like to move: "When I separated from your father, my brother helped me get the down payment. I bought this house, Angie. I worked hard to pay it off, and this is my house. And I like it here."

That person from the crew just saw a three-bedroom house with one bathroom and a little driveway in the middle of what she considered nowhere. She was looking down on the woman that I have looked up to my whole life. I say this to you and I mean it: **Don't let anybody dim the shine of your accomplishments. If they're not paying your bills, why in the hell would they validate your worth?** I watched my mom work so hard to have the money to raise four kids by herself without ever again depending on a man. She was always juggling two jobs—a nursing gig here, a school thing there. When she was home, my mother didn't have time to be anything but a disciplinarian, making sure that we were clean, getting good grades, and always going to church.

We lived across the street from our church, Breeding Tabernacle. My mom's feeling was, "If those doors are open, y'all is gonna have your asses in there." Sho' nuff, as she would say, and with no lip. "Go on over there." If we ever said we were bored, her response was, "Are you being lazy? Because I don't have no lazy children."

My happiest memories of my mother are in the kitchen on the Saturdays she could be home. She would be in there cooking all day

while she put us to *work* cleaning the house. She had everyone up
and at 'em with Pine-Sol and bleach, scrubbing everything. To this
day, I have to have that Pine-Sol smell in my house. That's how I
know it's clean. But now I have a housekeeper, okay?

Even with four kids, my mother stretched the generosity of her
heart to take in another from time to time. My dear cousin Dana
from South Bend used to spend the summers with us. We were born
two days apart, and she was like the baby sister I never got to have.
Mom has this ceramic set she uses as decoration, hanging in the
kitchen for all to see. A giant fork and spoon arranged with the
Lord's Prayer on a plaque in the center. It's like Jesus's coat of
arms, I guess. We weren't supposed to even touch it.

"Y'all running around this house playin'," Mom yelled at us.
"If y'all break my ceramic set . . . Lord, there will be nothing left of
you."

We were running, and Mom was at work. Dana did this whirl and
bumped right into the spoon. It was slow motion: The ceramic set
teetered, and tottered, and then finally fell forward. Miracle of mir-
acles, Dana caught it. But we were all screaming so much that the
poor girl got scared. In slow motion, we saw her lose hold of the
spoon, and the whole thing fell to the floor with a crash.

The Lord's Prayer popped out, and with it our lives, we were sure.
There was a dent in the wood. "You are gonna get a whipping!" my
brother Marvin yelled.

Dana burst into tears, hyperventilating and making a sound like
"Vitt vitt, vitt vitt." We were certain we were all dead. Mom came
home that night, and was sure enough furious. She didn't whip anyone. It was like her heart was so broken she couldn't bear to do it.
Mom had, and still has, a gift for making sure you know if she is
disappointed in you. Dana didn't get that whipping, but she got a
new name. To this day, we still call her Vitt Vitt.

When I was about ten, Mom got a really good job working at Eli

Lilly, the big pharmaceutical company in Indianapolis. She was proud of working there as a tech, getting to the plant early, staying late. She still wasn't able to give us as much time as she would have wanted to, but she was a provider. That was how she showed her affection, making sure we were secure. And she wanted us kids, especially me and Sugie, to know that no one would ever give us anything. I am thankful to this day that she instilled her work ethic in me. My friends make fun of me: "Why do you work so damn much, Vivica? You can pay that light bill." Yes, I can. And I always want to have that financial freedom, just like my mother did.

But that work ethic does come with a price. And maybe you're paying it in your own life. It's really hard for me to let people do things for me sometimes. Does that sound familiar? Whether it's the weight of emotional baggage or a carry-on suitcase, I'm always saying, "I got it, I'm strong. I can do it." It's only recently, as I've grown more comfortable in my skin as a single woman, that I have been able to simply say a gracious "Yes, thank you" to an offer of help.

We Fox kids threw ourselves into every extracurricular activity there was. At Arlington High, I wanted to be the best at track, volleyball, and cheerleading. And, of course, basketball. I was also very open to finding surrogate parents in my teachers, like Mrs. Fletcher, the teacher mom of my friend April. She spoke in such a dignified, kind manner. Her husband was also a teacher, and from six years old to senior year of high school, I spent a lot of afternoons in their home after school. It was the biggest, nicest house I'd ever seen black people have. They were always in teaching mode, and taught me to really notice my surroundings. When you went for a walk with them, you didn't just go by a tree.

"What do you notice about the tree, Angie?" Mrs. Fletcher once asked me.

"It has yellow flowers."

"That's right," she said. "It's a tulip poplar, the state tree of Indiana."

I'd walked by that tree countless times. Now it was special.

My daddy moved around a lot, but we spoke on the phone weekly and he came to all my games. He had a way of getting my attention and quietly coaching me, especially during basketball. I played power forward, where you have to be tough and play offense, but also make a quick turn to defense and shut down an opposing player. I had so much energy and took every game so seriously that he could tell before anyone else when I was getting too hyped. "Hey, chill out," he'd say. "Chill out." The phrase he used was "Attack intelligently." If I got too hyped out, the other team could capitalize on that. So whenever he saw me spaz out, his "Chill" was code for "Play your defense, listen to your coach. Attack intelligently."

I will never forget the time he showed up once with a pair of high-top gold Converse sneakers for me. I was so proud of them shoes. He started buying me more shoes for sports to encourage me. He got me so many sneakers that I once packed two left shoes in my gym bag for an away game at another school. It was a big basketball game—one that could get us into the Indianapolis Girls City Championship—so I *panicked* when I opened my bag just before the game and saw what I'd done. But I put them on and tried to make a joke out of it with my team. What could I do but do my best?

And it *was* one of the best games I had, maybe because I had to prove to the other team that I wasn't a damn fool with two left feet. My coach, Miss Maxine, she said after, "Foxy, you need to wear them two left shoes more often."

We went on to win the city championship. Indianapolis did us right, making a huge deal of our school's victory with an award ceremony. My father came, but not my mother, and all I remember is that I was a bucket of tears. I was so proud of the team. I also wished my mom had come.

Years later, I took Dad to a Pacers game and we got to sit right on the floor. He looked up behind him and put his arm around me. "Wow, from way up in section nine to down here sittin' on the floor." I also took him to the Super Bowl in 2012, the first time it was ever held in Indiana. I was thrilled, but unfortunately my dad ended up flirting with the lady beside us. I was like, "Dad, can you please focus on the damn game?"

He was always a ladies' man. Always. I definitely got my horndog nature from him. Because we were of like minds, I could always talk about boys and even matters of sex with my dad. I remember when I was in my twenties and dating all six-feet-eleven inches of Elden Campbell from the L.A. Lakers, I turned to my dad for advice on some concerns I had about fidelity. It was my first kind of public relationship, and I didn't want to look stupid with everyone watching. I would ask him, "Dad, what does it mean when he does this?" Or tell him, "He disappeared on me for a little while." And my daddy would say, "And did you two get into it? Okay, then he might be doing a little somethin' somethin', but you stay strong. If he really like ya, he'll come on back. And if he don't, you a good-lookin' girl—you my child." My dad's approach to trouble in a relationship was simple, and this is a direct quote: "The best way to get over that is with another pair of thighs. Keep it movin'. If he don't like you, he don't get you. Keep it movin'."

My mother's approach to disappointment in relationships was to do a love lockdown on her heart; my dad's go-to was to find the next person. They each decided the goal for me in love: Don't get hurt. My parents simply had different ways of showing me how to go about it. For better or worse—for richer or poorer (LOL)—in relationships, we can unconsciously repeat the patterns that we saw growing up.

Our little corner of Indianapolis was all I really knew of life, but my brother Marvin was about to spark the beginnings of my plan to see the world. We ended up calling him Sarge because he enlisted in the military as soon as he turned eighteen. It was during peacetime, thank God, 1978. We have the same July birthday four years apart, so I'd just turned fourteen. Since we share a birthday I sometimes joke that we're twins. He has my energy but goes about it in a quieter way.

The army came to get him so early in the morning. I watched from the front window, seeing my mom hugging him and kissing him good-bye. And she was *crying*, barely able to speak. It was sad, and yet we were so proud of him in that uniform that we were happy, too.

"I'll be back," he kept saying. "And I promise I will stay in touch and I'll write." Marvin and I always wrote to each other wherever he was in the world. It was so exciting for me to get his letters, filled with stories about being in Germany and Turkey. He went everywhere.

He was still in the army a few years later when I was trying to make it in California. Some new girlfriends wanted to show me a good time, so they took me to *Soul Train*. I did the line, dancing my heart out in a gray dress I thought would look cute on TV.

I got a letter from Marvin a little bit after the episode aired. "WAS YOU ON *SOUL TRAIN*?!?" were the first words, huge. He said he was watching TV with some of his boys and he started screaming, "That's my sister! That's my baby sister! Oh my God, it's Angie." That was the first time I was ever on TV, and I thank God I was able to share that moment with my Marvin.

But for now I was still in Indiana while Marvin saw the world. I started to see a little bit of it, at least. When my mom did get time off, we would take road trips down to see her family in Mississippi. It was *country as hell*. Huge acres of good ol' corn and greens and to-matoes. Her family always had lots of land. They had horses and cows and they rode on tractors and all that craziness. And I never felt more citified than when I was standing in Aunt Katherine's cow pasture with my cousins Baba Sue and Darryl. "Hmm, this is cute, Mom," I'd say. "When are we leaving?"

It was the trips to see family in Chicago that I loved, particularly to visit my aunt Corinne, or, as I and everyone else called her, Madame King. She owned a salon on the South Side, Madame King's Hair Fashions. She was fabulous and one of the first African Americans in Chicago to own her own salon. She loved makeup and had that hair, honey, with the blond highlights in it.

And she turned out to be my fairy godmother. It was in Madame King's storefront salon, a palace to a kid, that I first started reading movie magazines. There were tales of beautiful people doing extraordinary things with their lives. *Ebony* magazine's ads featured gorgeous black women looking right at the camera—right at me.

I was reading one of Madame King's magazines the summer I was thirteen, just before starting high school. Her big eyes suddenly shone on me.

"Angie, do you want to be in a fashion show?"

I didn't give her a half second, in case she changed her mind. "Yes, ma'am."

"Then come here, baby, we gonna cut your hair."

I put myself in Madame King's hands and was never the same. She cut my hair short, a pixie with a little bit of a shag, leaving it a little bit longer in the back. Oh, I was fine with that hairdo. And I walked in that fashion show, moving my arms exactly the way Madame King had told me. I can't for the life of me remember what I wore, but I remember smiling at the audience, and all of those faces smiling back. I got bit by the entertainment bug, compliments of Madame King.

I decided then and there that I was going to be a model. What was there not to like? You got onstage and everyone was looking at *you*. And you got to wear great clothes and be in magazines. You were fabulous. Why not be fabulous for a living?

I started high school with that haircut and I made the cheerleading team. They were like, "Ooooh, Angie Fox, that haircut is bangin'."

"Got it in Chicago," I would always say demurely, with a pat to my hair.

It was then that I started telling people, "I'm going to be a star." The response was not encouraging.

"Angie Fox, you ain't going nowhere."

But I kept telling people, "I'm going to be a star. You'll see." I just needed to figure out how.

Now, here's what I want to warn you about setting a goal. The bigger the dream, the more likely people will tell you not to try. There are three types of people who will try to hold you back. There's the basic motherfuckers who don't want to see you succeed—that's one group. They're the easiest to ignore, and actually you can use their "power" to inspire you to show them how wrong they are. (We'll talk about them later in Lesson 8. They can take a seat until we call for them.)

The second group doesn't want to see you get hurt, and so they want you to lower your expectations for what life can hold. These are the toughest to handle, because they think they are doing the right thing. They truly do care about you and are afraid to see you stick your neck out and get hurt. You have to be grateful for their concern, but you can't allow them to limit you.

And the last group, the worst, is scared to see you succeed. I call them the kind of company that loves misery! When I created *Vivica's Black Magic*, the Lifetime show chronicling the journey of creating a Las Vegas residency for male exotic dancers, I was working with this particularly fine young man. His baby mama had no interest in him—except his child support—until he started getting a little bit of attention and fame. He was a fan favorite even before the show came out, and people who follow me on Instagram saw that I was throwing him a little support and so they did the same. He started getting a ton of followers, and his ex saw him start to pull away from the pack and make it. Instead of giving support, she was suddenly saying, "No, come back here with me." She wanted him to give up the work that was obviously getting results. If he failed, she succeeded. She was relentless in this newfound interest in him, and I told him that for his sake he just needed to stop responding.

"But she calls me from numbers I don't know!" he said, desperate.

"Then don't answer your phone, period, child," I said. "Focus."

These people don't want to see you pursue your dream. These are also the types who want to keep you single. They don't want you to have a healthy relationship, because then who could they feel superior to?

Or maybe they are in the cubicle next to you at work, bitching about their job but not doing anything about it. Do you think they want to see you send out a résumé or ask for an informational interview at a dream job? Nope. They want you sitting right next to them so they have someone to bitch to.

It's the classic crab-in-a-bucket mentality: "If I can't have it, neither can you." Put a mess of live crabs in a pot, and on their own, each could escape, but instead they pull each other down again and again.

If you're finding yourself surrounded by those crabs, check yourself. Your squad needs an upgrade.

GET YOUR SQUAD TOGETHER— YOU'LL NEED THEM

Now, I'm sorry if you have a lot of school pride, but Arlington High was the best school of all time. I would put my school up against anybody's. The teachers demanded excellence, and we students expected each other to live up to Arlington Golden Knights standards. It was an almost all-black school at the height of the disco-funk era, and students would show up to school dressed to kill. People were like, "Ooh, the fine girls are over at Arlington." And they were right. *Everybody* used to look good.

Especially Reesie, who was a good friend of mine. I loved me some Reesie because the girls were all jealous of her. Reesie was *so* good-looking. She couldn't walk two feet without some fool girl trying to fight her.

But she took shit from nobody. I remember one day I heard this big commotion right after school. I turned a corner and saw Reesie fighting three girls. And she was hanging! The girls all left like it was their choice and they didn't just get their asses handed to them. Reesie was adjusting her clothes.

"Damn, girl, you're *fine*," I said. "What you fighting like that for?"

She didn't answer me. I didn't understand that the thing that made her stand out also made her a target for insecure people. But she refused to shrink from it or become invisible. God had made her beautiful, and she wasn't going to let haters dim her light.

Reesie was an important part of my Indy squad. A squad is that all-important group of friends who support you and motivate you to shine. I also had my girls Sheila and Bev, my skating rink buddies. I had mastered roller-skating at USA East, and we would get our outfits together so we could show off. Baby, we did not mess around. We would get song lyrics pressed on our shirts, in the old-style funky letters. My favorite said, "Have a funky good time." It was like our cute little uniform, and we would make sure our jeans were pressed with the same ultimate creases in them.

We all lived around each other, so I'd drive them over to the rink in my family's brown Cutlass Supreme. And that car had to be clean because whether we were going to USA East or the state fair, it had to be on like the Oscars red carpet. You had to *arrive*. Your whitewalls had to be spotless, the rims shiny, the black tires still gleaming from the Armor All you just put on.

Our squad would turn it out for Arlington's basketball games, which were a big deal for our part of Indianapolis. Our rival high schools were Broad Ripple and North Central—those matches got the biggest turnout and felt special, with all of our hopes aimed at that one shot, that one winning basket. Game days we'd be all dressed up in our Arlington Golden Knights gold, with me in my little gold cheer uniform. I never missed a game since I was a cheerleader for the boys and then I'd be bringing it home on the girls' team.

The games were a nice place for my girlfriends and me to meet boys, of course. I was in my element, totally confident. And junior year everyone was talking about the hot boys from Tech. There were these twin basketball players, Erwin and Derwin, who all the girls talked about. "Oohhh, baby, them twins right there," we cheerleaders would whisper to each other. God, I had a crush on Erwin.

Tech wasn't a rival, so it was fine for everyone to hang out after the game. Erwin came up to me, all tall and gorgeous. And we just started hanging out. He was a totally nice, sweet guy. We could drive around and talk about everything. I was my mama's good Fox girl, so our dates were always PG, but I swear to God I can't say the name "Erwin Shields" without letting out a sigh of happiness.

My dates were PG because Sug and I had a lot of friends who were getting pregnant. Just hot kids sneaking off and doing what comes naturally but with nobody telling them about safe sex or how exactly you can get pregnant. I watched classmates start having kids at thirteen and fourteen years old. The majority of my girlfriends got pregnant, in fact, and I watched their struggle and knew it was not for me.

I was on a basketball court when one of my girlfriends told me she was pregnant. This was junior year. My first instinct was to tell her I was sorry.

"I'm not sorry," she said. "I'm going to raise my baby with Kenny." Kenny was the boyfriend who only treated her like she existed every other day. The rest of the week he was on to some other girl.

"Okay," I said, with no judgment in my voice. I don't look down on a sister unless I'm helping her up. "Does he know?"

"Not yet," she said.

She wanted to hold on to that dream a little longer, I think. Guess what? Learning he was going to be a father didn't magically make Kenny, a kid himself, a better person. She raised that baby in her parents' house.

I would say that was the attitude of half of my friends who got pregnant. They thought it would help them keep a man. The other half was like, "Oh, shit."

That's the half that Sug and I paid attention to as our friends kept popping those babies out. They were stuck then. We said, "No, ma'am," to that. I've got to have some money and have me some fun. Ain't no way to do either sitting here having a bunch of babies. Sug told me not to mess with boys, if only for fear of the wrath of Everlyena Fox, who would tell it to you straight: "You're not bringing up a bunch of kids in yo' mama's house! You'll have to find someplace else to raise that baby."

What I admire about Sug is that it could have been something she handled. She had been looking after kids since she was little—why not stay comfortable with what you know? Having a baby grounded a lot of my friends where they were, and it was a reason not to have to pursue their dreams.

Sundays were all about church, and our pastor, Reverend Arthor McClendon, delivered the Word. He was a gentle soul and always positive, never delivering fire from the pulpit unless he felt it was absolutely necessary. Obviously, Reverend McClendon knew my dad wasn't around, and he quietly became a sort of secondary father to us Fox kids. He knew how we were doing at school and would urge us to stay focused on our studies. He had a wonderful sense of humor and smile. I spent so much time with him and his family, and I didn't miss a day of vacation Bible school during school breaks. And you know I sang in the damn choir. That's right, volleyball practice, track, basketball . . . and there's Angie Fox running over to Breeding Tabernacle for choir practice. Me and my girls Natalie, Sharon, and Georgia, we got all the solos.

My favorite to sing then, and a hymn that transports me still, is "Wade in the Water." Sing it with me for one second. "Wade in the water / Waaaaaaade in the water, children / Wade in the water / God's gonna trouble the water." It was not lost on us that this was a song important to the African American community. It's said the hymn was created as a coded message to assist the Underground Railroad, urging fugitive slaves to cross rivers so that the hellhounds of slave trackers lost their trail. An angel had "troubled" the water, waved his hand in it, and whoever entered that water would be freed of sin.

I thought about that beautiful song, and all the hours I spent at Breeding Tabernacle, while I was on the campaign trail for Hillary Clinton. I had campaigned for Barack Obama, so they knew I was a worker bee. In 2012 my friend BJ Coleman and I knocked on doors for him and went around to all the union halls. I passed out coffees to people waiting in line to get into rallies. It was fun and so rewarding to feel like I was part of something so much greater than just me.

Every time President Obama sees me, he is so kind. He says in this excited voice, "Hey, Vivica!" And everyone looks at me like, "Whaaaat?" My heart leaps with pride, I assure you. He is just so cool, and his family is a shining example of American excellence. So when Hillary asked Angela Bassett and me if we would help go around South Carolina to get out the vote, I said, "Of course, Madam Secretary." I thought, *It's only a few days.* Besides, I believed in her vision.

Well, by the second day I was so tired. Like, "God, I can't believe I signed up to do this" kind of tired. That afternoon, after morning shows, radio interviews, and meet-and-greets, we visited some historically black colleges and universities to talk to young people. I ended up on a panel with some older gentlemen who had marched for civil rights all those years ago.

As they shared stories about being beaten and sprayed and attacked by dogs, I just started crying. One guy talked about walking three miles to school, and his parents got up and walked with him so that he wouldn't get murdered by some asshole just because of the color of his skin. And the whole time they let him know to be grateful that he was going to school.

As they were talking, I looked out on all these beautiful young faces of Generation Next in the audience. And I thought to myself, *Thank you, God, that I got up today and* got out of my own way. *I am so blessed to be here right now, and I have to give back.*

Then I thought, as I go up to speak, *Now go tell 'em.*

"You guys are all our future leaders," I said to the audience. "Our future first ladies, our future presidents, our future lawyers, our future mothers, our future preachers. You guys go next. And it's so important for me to let you all know that you matter, that you count."

You matter, too. You count, too. I'm taking you to church here, I know. For me, focusing on my relationship with my Lord Jesus Christ has strengthened my resolve to be my best self. I want to experience all the blessings that He has for me. The lesson is not that you need to become Christian to get ahead—that turns my faith into some sort of get-rich-quick scheme. I'm just saying you at least have to believe in *yourself.* Look at the blessings you have, accept them with gratitude, and in return work to use those gifts.

If I'm really preaching anything with this book, it's that positivity works. Surround yourself with good people who want you to succeed, and once you do, give back and help the next generation along. I have seen some people live and fail with this foolish notion that strengthening others somehow weakens them. They live closed off in a fearful "I've got mine" mentality. If you have negative friends and negative habits, how can you expect positive results?

My friends from high school and church formed my Indy squad, and I still draw on the love and support that I found as a little girl. But nobody I knew had quite the same dream as me. There was no one to team up with on reaching my goal of being a star.

And then Pam Grier walked into my life with her gorgeous self. Well, not really. Some local affiliate played *Foxy Brown*, the classic 1974 film in which Pam poses as a prostitute to take down a "modeling agency" that's really selling women into sex slavery. I was transfixed. As Foxy, Pam was sexy, and beautiful, and tough. She could kick your ass in that red cutout jumpsuit.

None of us Fox kids were into TV—we'd rather be outside or at a game—but I leaned in watching *Foxy Brown*, marveling at this vision of what was possible. I began to model my demeanor on the blend of strength, smarts, and beauty of this unapologetically powerful black woman, the first I ever saw on television. She became my shero.

Years and years later I got a chance to interview Pam for a BET special. I could barely make it through the interview, I was crying so damn much. She had been my imaginary friend for so long, my "squad goal." I'd even named my production company Foxy Brown Productions in tribute to her.

"I just . . . thank you," I said. "Thank you for being such a role model to me all of my life. I would not be who I am without you."

"Baby, that's what I'm here for," she said, so graciously, taking my hand to make sure I understood that she meant it. "To pass the torch to you, to inspire you so you know you can do it."

With Pam as my life goal, I had begun to build my own squad, even if they were imaginary friends. I added Diana Ross and Michael Jackson to my little group of fantasy mentors when I got to see them in concert when I was a junior in high school. If Pam showed me the presence and grit of a movie star, that night Diana showed me that a black woman could literally be the most glamorous person in the whole world. Miss Ross changed clothes six times, each gown more extravagant than the last, and I had never seen a black woman with hair and nails like that. She sang "It's My House," reeling off all the little luxuries she had put in her home. She was rich not because of some man, but because she had earned every dime. She was simply the most beautiful woman I'd ever seen. That really stayed with me.

And then there was Michael, who showed me the power of entertainment. He came out to dance with her during "Upside Down." He was magic—that's the only word to describe it. They delighted in each other onstage, holding the entire audience in their grip. And to a little black girl like me, the message was clear: "Look how talented and cool we *all* are. You are part of this. You are special."

Michael and Diana showed me models of what was *possible*. I'd put Diana Ross songs on and do little runway shows in my house, feeling she would approve of every supermodel turn of my face or hip. I used Michael's music as I exercised. I'd decided my calves were a little too bitty for a would-be athlete-model like myself, so I'd jump rope to *Off the Wall*, both sides of the record, with little weights on my ankles to build up and tone my calves. And I dreamed that Michael would be so impressed with my dedication.

This is a flash-forward, but I will tell you that one of my very first gigs was as an extra in Michael's "Remember the Time" video. You didn't see me? You sure? Well, my arm makes a stunning cameo when Iman pushes away a servant's offer of tea. "That's my arm!" I screamed to my friends when the video premiered on MTV. "That arm right there!"

It didn't matter that I was an extra. I didn't care. I got to sit there all day and watch Michael Jackson dance. He was the most amazing thing I've ever seen in my life. What I remember most is how he could pick up that choreography; because he's very quiet, he'd barely nod as they went over it. He was just Michael, to himself. Then the director, John Singleton, would say, "Okay, y'all, here we go. One . . . two . . . three . . ." And it was like somebody turning on a light switch. As Michael was hitting those moves, it was like, BAM, BAM, BAM.

When he passed in 2009, I had lived with Michael in my mind for so long. He was the king of my imaginary squad. I legit cried for three days.

Junior year I started getting my own entertainment magazines, looking for any stories on Diana and Michael. There was one about Michael recording at his home studio in Encino, California. I knew from all the Indiana coverage that the Jacksons had lived in Gary, just two hours north of where I was reading on my bed. Now he was living in a mansion with white shag carpeting, chandeliers, gates . . .

Michael had made a wish and made sure it was a big one that he had to live up to. He got out, and it was like he was saying through the photo, "Angie, come to California." To live the life of my dreams, I needed to be in a place that had room for big dreamers.

Now, instead of just telling people I was going to be a star, I had a plan: "I'm going to California, and I'm going to be famous."

"Angie Fox, you might go there," they'd say, "but you'll be right back."

My Arlington High classmates were making college plans, and the question kept coming at me my senior year of high school. Teachers and people at church were all asking, "Angie, where are you going to college?" I was like, "I'm not. I'm going to California. I'm gonna make it."

There were head shakes, pleas, tut-tuts. Finally my mother couldn't take it. She told me I had to go to college and that was it. So let's say I negotiated. I found a two-year program at Golden West College in Huntington Beach, California. It would allow me to study part-time while I pursued modeling. It was the deal I had to make.

By now you know my mom. Once I convinced her to let me go to California, she was like, "Unh-unh, you not going out there broke." So I got my first job at Burger Chef. It was an Indianapolis-based chain, and I did the counter and the takeout: "Welcome to Burger Chef, can I take your order?" This is when drive-thrus were starting to take off, so it was actually a cool job to have in town. I also had my first boss, Lee, who was so cool. He wasn't one of those hovering bosses who's mean. "Go on out there, girl," he'd say. "You get those cheeseburgers ready for 'em." I don't know if he knew money was tight or if he was just nice, but he would tell me I could bring food home to my family at the end of the night. So you know they couldn't wait for me to get off work! "Yup, bring me that mushroom-and-Swiss burger," my big brother Sandy would say.

I realized I loved working and being a provider when I came home. Every single paycheck brought me closer to California, the land of my heroes.

Okay, I want you to do something for me. Think about the people who inspire *you*. Your fantasy mentors like Pam and Diana. The folks who are living the dream you want or who have the qualities you would like to present in tough situations. They could be famous, or they could be the owner of the company where you work. But they're people you'd love to meet for a coffee—or margaritas—just so you can get their advice.

I'll tell you the people that I find myself thinking of a lot lately: Michelle Obama, Sophia Loren, Diahann Carroll, and Tina Turner. I admire strong women, obviously. And I especially draw on the experiences of women whose careers expanded over a long time. These women looked at what worked and what didn't work for them, and they continued to flourish. They embody my motto: **Don't get older, get fucking better.**

I thought of Michelle and Diahann when I was on *Celebrity Apprentice*, having a boardroom confrontation with a lesser woman. I called upon the spirits of these great women, trying to embody their grace and directness. And do you know what happened? Right after it aired I got a call from Lee Daniels, the brilliant director and creator of *Empire*, the biggest show on TV. He saw that Michelle and Diahann in me and wanted it for his show.

So thank you, spirit squad, for backing me up. They helped me tell that toxic trick to keep it moving *and* got me one of my favorite gigs, *Empire*. And I got to work with one of my sister girls, Taraji P. Henson. I am so proud of her journey, and I was touched to find out that I had once been part of *her* imaginary squad, in the same way that Pam Grier was for me. "I watched Vivica before I even got into the business," she told *Entertainment Weekly* when *Empire* announced I was joining the cast. "And she's always been one that I've looked up to, like, 'God, I want to be able to do what she does.' So, to be able to work with the person who you've admired for so long, it's just mind-blowing." I'm quoting that article not to brag—okay, I let it go on—but to show you that everyone, even the incredibly gifted Taraji P. Henson, can benefit from finding a role model and saying, *I want to do what she does. Let me do the work.*

For practical purposes, it's important to reach out to mentors in real life. One of the people I was desperate to work with coming up was Queen Latifah. Getting to be with her on the set of *Set It Off* was such a learning experience. Here she had this phenomenal rap career, and then managed to become the star anchor of a sitcom I loved, *Living Single*. And then she bursts out of that box to be a movie star. We actually had to map our production Wednesday through Sunday to get around Latifah's schedule. But she was 100 percent committed. She would be asleep in her makeup chair because of it, getting cornrows. I was like, *This girl is even multi-tasking sleep!* Watching her helped me define what was possible—and smart—in not being limited or typecast.

Another mentor for me has been Sean "P. Diddy" Combs. He'll always be Puffy to me. Talk about an entrepreneur spirit. Hanging out with him, I soaked in so much knowledge about branding and diversifying. Yes, he was a rapper and producer. But that was only the way in the door. He would tell me about clothing lines, liquors, and colognes. He wasn't simply helping to sell someone's project. He was producing the product and employing people while still staying true to his fan base. That's how you become the boss.

I took their lessons to heart. I sing, I act, I dance, and I will always love entertainment. But my true brand is quality. Whether they're buying something from the Vivica Fox Hair Collection or selecting an item from my clothing line, I want people to be as satisfied as they are in a kick-ass performance. The biggest takeaway from Puffy as an entrepreneur is that sleep is optional. Work hard, sleep later.

So invite people you'd like to meet to join your squad of supporters and mentors. **Don't be afraid to contact people who are successes in the field you want to excel in.** Trust, they are proud of what they've achieved and they *want* to share how tough it was—and that last part will give you an advantage when you face those same obstacles. Someone might advise you to get a specific license it took them years to figure out they needed, or to set up a credit card payment system for clients so you're not chasing checks later. Boom— you learned their lessons at no cost to you.

Think big, too. Go after leaders in your field. You want greats like Queen Latifah and Puffy. Don't class yourself down and talk to the assistant's assistant out of fear that you're not worthy of someone's time. You damn sure are. Go right to the leader. Once you talk, you can ask to shadow them for a day, or meet in their office for an informational interview about their work. It definitely won't happen if you don't ask.

Closer to home, I want you to ask yourself who in your circle of friends can help you on the regular? Who can support you as you reach for these goals? It can be as easy as sharing that dream with a trusted friend *or* someone new who can offer you a fresh perspective. Either way, you are creating a support network you can turn to so it's not you all the time providing the momentum. They can hold you accountable for small and big goals. Let's say you dream of starting your own hair salon. If you tell yourself, *This week I'll look at spaces and maybe do some recon on places that opened in the last year or so,* then *maybe* you'll do it. Or your other work and family responsibilities might take precedence. But tell your friend you're going to do something and you are far more likely to do your homework. You won't want to tell her, "Yeah, about that. I did squat."

For me that go-to person is my wonderful business partner Lita Richardson. She is the one I turn to when I need to ask myself, *Okay, what are the next goals? What is possible that I'm not seeing, me myself?*

I first met Lita at a Magic Johnson event at Paramount Studios back when I was getting my hustle going as an actress. We were just two women at the bar, chilling by ourselves and absorbing the scene. Lita had a cute short haircut, and she is so beautiful that I assumed she was also an actress or model. I told her I liked her hair and I asked what type of work she did.

"I'm a lawyer," she said.

"*You're* a lawyer?!" I yelled, not able to hide my surprise. All the lawyers I'd seen were old white guys. "What kind of law?"

"Entertainment law," she replied.

We would see each other at events and for some reason I could never remember her name. So I would say, "The pretty lawyer!" when I ran into her. I was starting to work a lot, and as I got more gigs, I realized it made sense for me tax-wise to get incorporated. I asked Lita to help me with that, and she later became my business partner. She always advises me and makes sure I read my contracts and know what the hell I am signing up for.

We check in usually once or twice a week. I get people trying to come at me sideways, "How about you invest in this?" And I always run it by Lita. She'll hear an idea or look over a contract for me. "Nope, you shouldn't do that," she might say. Or if I really want something, she helps me make sure my bases are always covered and I protect myself. Lita has been with me so long that she is also my reality check. Whenever I get too comfortable in a job or take a blessing for granted, she is there to say, "Hey, missy, appreciate this." She can say that because she was also there to lift me up when sure-bet shows got canceled or a movie I was dying to do sputtered in development. You need that someone to encourage your grind.

Lita actually brought me the opportunity to take over a line of wigs by Beverly Johnson, the legendary fashion icon who was the first African American model to ever appear on the cover of *Vogue*. I said to Lita, "All the damn money I've spent on wigs and weaves. Let me get some of those chips back." Besides, I had been waiting for exactly this kind of opportunity. Back in the day, I had a stylist, a nice Swiss girl named Petra, who also worked with Raquel Welch, the number one wig seller in the world. One day I was with Petra, and I saw racks and racks of clothes.

"What the hell is all that?" I asked.

"Oh, that is for Raquel's big wigs shoot," Petra answered in her deep Swiss voice.

"Damn," I said, "how many changes does she do?"

"Oh, Vivica, we shoot for a couple of days and work all day," she said, then added in a conspiratorial whisper, "But she makes so much money with that wig stuff."

So when Lita hit me up with the Beverly Johnson opportunity, I yelled, "Sign me up! Sign my ass up right now!" But the Johnson line was in sad shape when I came on the scene. The way they were styling the wigs was boring and tired. They weren't involved. "Look here, we gonna make this sexy," I said. "We gotta make it like Puffy does with Cîroc—we gotta make it not about the wig, but about a lifestyle. We gotta let girls know that to wear wigs isn't that big of a deal."

I had to laugh when I quickly saw one blog, some hater, saying, "Now she's selling wigs. Hmm. When the checks stop coming in . . ." The joke was on them. They didn't know the hair business is a billion-dollar-a-year thing. They didn't know that, but I did. *I* did my homework. Remember that when people are laughing at you for your business ideas.

The hair game has changed so much since I got in it, and I'd kind of like to take credit for it, to be very honest with you. You have great artists from Lady Gaga to Nicki Minaj come out rocking wigs. That inspires people to have fun and experiment. Then you have these young girls wanting to wear their braids down to their asses or have all these weaves in different colors. Well, guess who serviced 'em? Vivica did. The great part is that now everyone is trying to get into the hair game, or just doing lifestyle brands like Gwyneth Paltrow and the lovely Jessica Alba. And I beat them to it. Thank you, Lita.

So I really advise people: Get your Lita. I know that might sound easy to say to someone starting out, but at the very least there is nothing wrong with investing in yourself and getting a consult from a lawyer. Or at least getting a consult from a business-savvy friend until you can afford one. Whether you're buying a house or teaming with someone on a project, you can ask him or her to look at contracts and make sure you realize what you're signing up for. For years, women have been told to "sign and smile." Be grateful for the opportunity, don't negotiate, and don't ask questions.

But if you do it right, you're not just walking into that office or business opportunity alone. You've got a squad backing you up and pulling for you.

And I hope you'll include me.

DON'T LET ANYONE WORK HARDER THAN YOU

Just one month after high school graduation, I packed my bags for California. I was seventeen years old, and I felt like my life was finally starting. Before I left Indy, I went to see Reverend McClendon to get his blessing one last time. By then he knew my goal: I wanted to be a model and I really thought I could make it. I thanked him again for always being so positive.

"Stay out of trouble, now," the reverend told me.

"I will," I said.

"And Angie, don't you get involved with that crazy nightlife," he said. "California is going to be a big place. Make sure you don't get caught up with bad people."

"No, sir," I said.

Bright and early, Dad was there to drive me out west. He told me I always was his most adventurous child. "Eyes wide open yelling for me," he said, "ready to take in life like a big old sponge."

We took Route 66, and at one point I fell asleep. Keep in mind, Indiana is the flattest land on God's earth. So when I woke up to see mountains, I screamed.

"Dad, it's so beautiful!"

"Yes, baby," he said, in his seen-it-all voice, "we're in Colorado."

Next we drove through Las Vegas, which might as well have been Mars. We stopped at a light, and I saw a woman with that sky-blue eye shadow, leather skin, and blond hair, smoking all them cigarettes. "Dad, what's *up* with her?" I asked.

"Oh, baby, that's them Vegas people right there," he said, like we were on safari. "You are looking at the genuine article."

When we got to Huntington Beach, I realized why all the stars lived in California. It was gorgeous, and nicknamed "Surf City" for the perfect waves and hot surfers. It had something else I wasn't used to. I mean, I was raised around white people, but Huntington Beach was kinda like, *Whoa, okay, it's a* whole bunch *of white people up in here.*

The deal was that I was going to stay with my brother Marvin's girlfriend at the time, Diana. Dad brought me to the apartment, and before he left, we both cried like babies.

Diana didn't really want to play tour guide to a kid sister—a sign of things to come with her—so I explored Huntington Beach on my own. I was looking at everything, breathing in the ocean air. This Indiana girl literally stepped off a sidewalk so she could touch her first palm tree. Like the Sister from Another Planet or some shit. I said aloud to no one but myself, "Well, that is a different type of tree right there."

And that ocean! It was the first time I'd ever seen the ocean, and I fell in love with its strength and beauty. After I met some other students, I remember, something we always did was end the night by swimming in the ocean. Now I am like, *What the hell was I think-*

ing? I could have been eaten by a shark! But when you're young, you just do stuff.

One of the things I knew I had to do was live on my own two feet. About a week after I got settled in California, I called my mother.

"You know, Mom," I said, "I don't want you to send me money."

She was quiet. Money was how she knew I was secure. "You sure, Angie?"

"I'm gonna go get a job because I can do schoolwork and I can do real work," I said. "I think knowing you're sending money will make me lazy."

I knew she would understand that. "Lazy" was a four-letter word for my mom. She stayed quiet.

"Let me earn," I said, "because I want to go do this for myself."

"If you need me, I'm always here," she said. I know now she was proud of that. Proud that she could provide, always that. But glad that she'd raised a worker.

But Lord, what had I done? Well, you know Everlyena Fox's daughter went and got a job right away. In fact, I got two. One was at a Waldenbooks store in the Huntington Beach mall and the other was at Famous Raymond's Potato Palace. (See, even then I knew to diversify my career.) The Palace had a—wait for it—all-baked-potato menu. Come on into my kitchen, and I can still make you a potato with broccoli and cheddar cheese, or chili and cheddar cheese, or meatballs and Parmesan cheese. And, of course, bacon bits, sour cream, and chives. Miss Vivica will make sure you get all the fixin's.

At the Potato Palace, I met this girl Melanie. We clicked right away, and I told her I'd only been living with Diana three weeks and I couldn't take it. I think she had designs on being a military wife. She had this life planned with Marvin that I knew my brother had no clue about. I flat-out told Melanie I couldn't stand living with Diana.

"Come live with my family," Melanie said.

I pictured a bunk bed or some sitch. "Oh, that's so nice of you . . ."

"We got an extra room if you don't mind paying rent." That was more like it. I didn't want charity and I needed my own space. And the rent was better than what I was paying, so it was "See ya, Diana!" (And yes, Marvin broke up with her right quick.)

I was building up my little California squad, adding two new friends, Lisa and Gigi. They were my party girls, the ones who took me to *Soul Train*. We would go to the Red Onion for margaritas. Melanie's family decided they were moving, and I ended up living with Gigi's family. They were Filipino and adored me. I was like a little foreign exchange student to them. Their pretty little black fake daughter. My Filipino mama was a great cook, especially with fish. But, oh God, they loved rice. They would eat it to death! And I'd eaten so much of it growing up that I'd had my fill for life. I am still in touch with these women today, and yes, I still call Gigi's mother Mom.

I realize now, of course, looking back, how I was protecting myself from feeling lonesome. Re-creating a family life was my way of feeling less scared on my little adventure.

I had plenty to be afraid of, frankly. Breaking into modeling was tougher than I ever expected. I would make an appointment with an agency, and each time I would think, *Well, here we go.* I had my little pictures all ready to show them. I'd walk in and the rejection was pretty quick, though they thought they were being kind.

"We already got a black girl," they'd say. "She looks just like you." Then, in a sort of throwaway gesture, they'd add, "You've got a great look."

I'd nod, thank them for their time, and see myself out. That was before the days of us coming in different shades and colors. They had their look and they were happy with their quota: one.

I needed some excitement to make up for selling books and potatoes while facing constant rejection. So I started venturing out to Los

Angeles, hanging out with more girls. I was discovering who I was, and that nightlife was calling me. Exactly like Reverend McClendon had warned me. I'd go out to L.A. with my new friends and party. It was amazing meeting all these new people, going out Saturday and not hearing Mama yelling on Sunday morning, "Time for church!"

I had a good run partying and living for weekends. Before I knew it, I was doing less and less work for my Golden West degree, and picking up more hours to fund the clubbing. Don't get me wrong and cue up the eighties *Less Than Zero* soundtrack. I never got messy or anything even like that. What I was guilty of was wasting time.

There was a moment where I had to do what I call "flipping the channel." I was out late one night at another club in L.A., and I kind of looked around at who I was hanging with. These weren't my homegirls or Gigi. They were people who liked to drink and be seen. And this one guy was eyeing me for a while. Then he got real close.

"You look like a model," he said. He was cute but, ooh, that gin-and-tonic breath.

It was the aha moment. *Like* a model. I wasn't one. I was thinking it was cute to have guys buy me drinks, thinking it mattered whether or not I was the prettiest girl in the place. That was acting *like* a model, not being one.

I gave the guy a polite smile and looked at all the people around me. These people weren't hustlers. They were not focused on anything other than getting a waitress's attention. *I am around people who are going nowhere and I am better than this*, I thought. *All this clubbing ain't equaling no paychecks! I need to switch things up here.* I had to buckle down and get it together.

I entered a few modeling competitions. One was called Face Finders, and I got to go to Arizona and was a finalist. All the girls were talking about wanting to go to New York. "That's where the best models go," one said.

A girlfriend of mine, Barb, wanted to get into the music business, and she kept bringing up New York, too. One day I turned to her. "Let's try it out," I said. "Let's move to New York."

Cut to us living in Hell's Kitchen. Our apartment was a dingy little hole near Times Square, back when Times Square was rough and dirty. Barb and I slept on two air mattresses on the floor. No matter how I scrubbed the place, it never felt like home. It was a romantic starving-artist scene, only there was nothing romantic or in the least bit nice about it. I called my mom as soon as I got a phone.

"I moved to hell, Mom."

"Well," she said, "you wanted to go there."

A friend from L.A. by the name of Jill Jones was also living in New York. She was the blonde in Prince's "1999" video, working the keyboard and grinding with Lisa from Wendy & Lisa. Prince loved her voice and they had a thing going. I thought it would be good for Barb to meet her, so I invited Jill over to our place.

"What the hell are you doing over here?" she said, standing in the doorway. "Vivica, I'm rescuing you."

She did. Prince had her put up in a penthouse across town by Grand Central. Since she was always traveling with Prince, she said I could live with her there for free. "Just take care of my dogs," she said. "I've got you."

Me and them two dogs were some pampered bitches. She had these two little Malteses, and we had a fine time acting like that penthouse was our place. It was like I'd moved from the projects to Beverly Hills. The place had white carpets and white walls, and I would take the most luxurious bubble baths in this huge tub. Even the water felt rich! I would come home from modeling look-sees and look out over the beautiful lights of the city. If I kidded myself enough, I could feel like I'd made it. But none of this was really mine. I was playing pretend, no different from Barbie in a dream house. I wasn't jealous, though. I felt, *One day I will earn this and have this, too.*

I lived like a princess for nearly a year, not paying rent, my career treading water in that pretty bathtub. Then one day Jill gave me a call.

"Hey, girl, me and him aren't going through good things right now," she said. With Prince, it was always "him." She didn't need to clarify.

"Oh, I'm sorry, baby," I said.

"I'm going to have to move, Vivica."

It was like the record scratched. If Jill moved, I moved. Prince was paying for my little fantasy and I'd never even met him. And when the relationship was over, it was like someone called the repo man on Jill. Girl, bye!

I made the mistake of becoming comfortable in someone else's success. I had to pull up stakes, but I was not going to Indianapolis, that's for sure. I decided to go back to Huntington Beach and Gigi's family so I could finish up school. (Which I did, thank you very much, Mom. I got my associate's degree in social and behavioral sciences.)

I took a cab to the airport, and my whole life could be crammed into two bags. I looked back at the skyline of Manhattan and I thought, *When I come back, I'm gonna be famous.* And I was. The next time I came to New York I was a bona fide soap opera star.

And yes, I finally met Prince in 2011. He invited me onstage to dance for him at his show at the Forum. He was a little bitty thing, but he had some moves! I was too busy dancing to thank him for all those bubble baths. His passing was a terrible shock, and I will always be indebted to him for giving me that first taste of real luxury.

Once I was back in California, there was no more time to mess around. I needed to be ready, to stay attentive for opportunity and ready to act immediately. No warm-up, no "let me think about it." I carried my modeling portfolio with me everywhere, expecting to be discovered and visualizing how I would react so I'd be able to take my moment and make it count. And I truly believe that because I put my intention out there, fate responded with an "I see you, girl."

It happened when I was having lunch with a girlfriend outside at Cravings, an Italian restaurant on Sunset Boulevard. I was wearing this leopard-print miniskirt with cowboy boots and a black shirt, and I had my hair up. This man came walking along the street and then stopped at our table to look right at me.

"Excuse me, are you an actress?" he asked, with a British accent.

"Noooo," I said, "but I'm a model." I went digging into my bag. "Would you like to see my portfolio?"

"No, but here's my number," he said. "My name is Trevor Walton. Please call me. I think you would be great for a television show I'm doing."

His card said he was a producer at Paramount. But the second he was gone, my friend, who was not in the entertainment business, was all like, "Okay, these guys out here are devils trying to get girls and turn them into prostitutes." If I called this Trevor, she said, I was basically signing my life away to the Hillside Strangler.

I listened to my instincts instead. This was the moment I had stayed ready for. And I later came to find out Trevor didn't want nothing from me but my talent. There was something in me that he saw. And he became my guardian angel. He got me an agent and an audition for a pilot at Paramount. When I went in, I didn't know what the hell I was doing. But I smiled, pushed aside my fear, and did it anyway. There is nothing as inspiring to an artist or entrepreneur as having nothing to lose.

Trevor called after the audition. "They said you were green," he told me. "Green as hell. But they all knew this was your first time and they liked you." I didn't get the job, but Trevor guaranteed me I'd be working.

I landed a Clearasil commercial where I had to run around on Melrose pretending I was getting chased by pimples. I didn't even have lines. There was someone yelling, "Don't let the zits get you!" But it was $400, scale, and you have to start somewhere.

Let me tell you how auditions go. It's rare that they ask you to sit down and talk about yourself. You might get that little tiny bit of sugar when you come in. Like, "Hello, what's your name?" Usually, it's "You got any questions? Okay, let's go." Sometimes you can feel the room, and you think, *Ooooh yeah.* You know they're with you.

Then they may give you some notes and ask you to try it a different way. That's to see if you're coachable. Just to see if you can give them a little something else. But most of the time it's "Thank you." You see yourself out and you wait by the phone.

You have to be sympathetic to the casting agent, who is kind of like a hiring manager or someone you see in HR. Maybe you think you're perfect for the job, but they have the whole film—or company—in mind. You have to be the right fit, so if you're hungry, your best bet is to go into your audition or interview and be flexible so they know you're coachable.

I kept working my day jobs while I auditioned, but I started working smarter, thanks to my "host sister," Gigi.

"Girl, you need to stop working these little jobs."

"What do you mean?" I asked. I liked the bookstore, and you know I loved the Potato Palace.

"You need to come work with me at Bob's Big Boy and be a real waitress."

"What's the difference?"

"You'd go home every day with *money*," she said.

"Whaaat?"

"Oh, yes, sweetie," she said with a laugh. "These tips flow *in* over there."

And so that's what got me from behind the counter and introduced me to the world of waitressing. I loved it. I felt like I was getting a grade at the end of the meal. That cash in hand was good, thank you,

Gigi. But I kept at my auditions, until I saw a notice that *Days of Our Lives* was casting. I went in with all those auditions under my belt, and I wasn't so green anymore. I'm no Michael Jordan, but he once said of a Nike commercial: "Why don't they show all the times I failed to get to success?" (Did you know he was cut from his high school basketball team? Stick *that* on your inspiration board!)

I'd had plenty of failures, so I was definitely ready for success. *Days* would be my first speaking role, and I wasn't going to have to pretend pimples were out to get me.

I was a nervous wreck the night before my first day on *Days of Our Lives*. I had my lines down cold, make no mistake, but I was worried about the five A.M. call time. I was still living in Huntington Beach, and I had to get to the NBC studio in Burbank. You can never guess how L.A. traffic will be. My friend Lisa Mapps had a place in L.A., and she was like, "Vivica, just sleep on my couch." So my major TV debut followed a night of couch surfing.

Everybody on set was really sweet, and I admit I was a little starstruck. These were people I'd seen on TV for years, and there they were, speed-reading scripts and checking their makeup. I have, to this day, the utmost respect for soap actors. Working on one is like acting boot camp since the schedule is so grueling. If your character has a story going, you do five shows a week, and then go home to memorize pages and pages of dialogue. And you have to make the most outlandish story lines real, all while hitting your mark and crying on cue.

One of the first things I learned was that nobody had time to wait for you to get teary for a crying scene. When I first had trouble, the crew was like, "Oh, baby, we've got a little trick for you." They blew menthol mist into my eyes, and that would make you tear up. That is why I said, "I gotta learn to cry on cue 'cause this shit stings like a mother."

I also learned about craft services. That's one thing about show business: You *will* get fed. 'Cause they got food everywhere. That's why you see actors and actresses get a little chubby when they finally get a job. You can't blame a once-starving actor for not being able to push away from the table, you know? Sometimes it's steak and lobster; other times—and this is a pet peeve of mine—wraps or some garbage. It all depends on how big the production is and how much the people in charge like to eat, too. At the soaps, there was always breakfast, because it was a twelve-hour day. On *Days*, you could go to the NBC commissary for lunch, and that was always fun. You would see stars from other shows, and it added to the community feel. We were all working actors, living our dreams.

I'd been in audition mode so long that I stayed that way. Every day I tried to earn my part on that show. I knew my lines; I knew my scene partners' lines. I showed up early; I stayed late. I wanted to be there even more, but the writers just weren't building up my story. *China Beach* called, and I'd landed a little arc on there as part of a makeshift girl group in Vietnam, the Candettes. But the thing that seemed like it could be the start of something even bigger was a small—and I mean small—role in Oliver Stone's docudrama *Born on the Fourth of July*. My character's name was "Hooker, VA Hospital," so that gives you a sense of my scene with Tom Cruise. As you know, Tom plays Ron Kovic, a paralyzed Vietnam War veteran, and I straddle another war vet in the hospital bed next to him. My lines were "Why, sure, sugar." "Like this?" "Anything you want, baby." I was a nice prostitute, thank you.

I was on set just one day, and it was overwhelming. I just wanted to not get fired, so I was just standing there and trying to not get in the way. I admit I was looking to see Tom Cruise. You know, that sexy Tom I knew from *Top Gun* and *Cocktail*. As I'm looking, this crew guy walked by me looking like a rough biker who needed a shave and a shower. He stopped right in front of me.

"Hi there," he said, holding out his hand.

"Hi," I said, shaking it kind of warily but so nervous about being on a film set that I would take anyone as a friend. I found myself looking into the most intense and most beautiful green eyes I had ever seen in my life.

"What's your name?" he asked.

I paused, drawn into those eyes. "My name is Vivica," I said. Did we have a fixer-upper on our hands here? I thought, *I can get him a razor* . . .

"Tom," he said. "Nice to meet you."

As he was walking away, I realized that was Tom Cruise.

"Oh my God," I said aloud. "Was that Tom Cruise?"

He heard me and turned back with that smile. "Yeah," he said, "I look kinda jacked up, huh?"

"Oh man!" So that was my first meeting with Tom Cruise. He was the most polite guy, and he was committed to work. He knew everyone's name on that crew, and I thought, *That's how a star acts.* **You can be humble and still be confident.** The biggest star in the world came right up to me and introduced himself to someone with three half-lines and a half day's work. To this day, I do that on every single set I'm on.

Meanwhile, *Days* still wasn't really putting much into my character. I was holding down my waitressing gigs, too. I didn't want to turn down good work like *China Beach* or opportunities to do small film roles if *Days* was going to cut me at any moment, so I asked for a contract.

They said they couldn't at the time, and I made a decision. "Oh well, gotta go, then."

If you feel you are not valued at work or not selling like you think you should, get real and think about why. Is it because you're not applying yourself? For me, working hard means going above and beyond, not simply doing what's in the job description. If you're in an

office or company, you've got to be a team player. That means coming in early, doing something extra, doing those little bitty things.
When you go out to get coffee, bring something for the boss. I'm
not saying be a kiss-ass or brownnoser, just prove you're a team
player.

Make it so that no one can say, "Well, are you qualified? You
weren't here, you haven't applied yourself, and you haven't done the
extra thing . . ."

If you've done all those things and you're still not moving up, then
you can walk away knowing your worth. **If you're not valued, move
on.** That's what I did with *Days*. I heard about an opportunity to join
Generations, the first soap opera centering on an African American
family, with the promise of a much bigger role than I had on *Days*. I
went for it and got the gig.

My *Generations* character, Maya Reubens, was a dance girl, and it
was fun to play her. The best day was when I found out Richard
Roundtree was playing my dad. Shaft is my dad? Lord, what? Richard Roundtree starred as a detective in the *Shaft* series, a collection
of films that has defined representations of black male power in movies for years. He's a bad motha— Shut your mouth! The story was
that Maya has been helping her father stay on the run for fifteen years
after a mysterious lab explosion. I brought *layers* to the work. I was the
costar that people would be like, "Shit, you don't want to do nothing
with Vivica because she will come in and steal that damn scene."

Still, I was new as an actress. I had my first love scene ever on *Generations*. It was with Kristoff St. John, who was the male lead of the
show. And I damn near ran out of the bed. I was like, *Oh, Lord Jesus,
what the hell is this?* I said, "We are *not* making out."

He was such a pro, but I was still a little bit Angie from Indy. *Everlyena's gonna kill me behind this one*, I thought. But I got through it.
When I first started acting, my impulse was always: *Oh my God, what's
my mother going to say?*

But again, you have to be ready to face your fears and do it anyway. Having courage doesn't mean you don't still get anxious. To this day, I get butterflies walking on a new set or stepping onto a stage. Not every now and again. I am talking *every single time*. Maybe you get anxious when you're giving a presentation, or meeting a new boss or client. **Butterflies just mean the work is still important to you.** And that's good.

Here's a tip for taming those nerves: When I get too in my head before a performance, I've learned to ask God for help. I say, *Give me grace, Lord, so that I can perform to the best of my God-given abilities. You have brought me to this point and I am grateful.*

And it works. Your whole life has brought you to that moment. Everything you've learned, all the hours you've put in, all that was training for the *now*. Remember that and you've got this.

Day to day on *Generations*, my on-screen dad, Richard, gave me such a sense of protection. One day we were working with a certain director. I won't bother you with his name because he wasn't a nice man and he's beneath your notice. At the time, I didn't know how little he thought of actors.

One day I asked the director a question. It wasn't a clichéd "What's my motivation?" question—I think it was about blocking or what beat I should enter the room on.

"Your job is to shut up and do what I told you to do," he spat.

I blinked. My instinct was to fight, but my other instinct was to keep my damn job. Like John Shaft incarnate, Mr. Richard Roundtree came to my rescue.

"*Your* fucking job is to direct her," he yelled. "You don't just tell her to shut up. She asked you a question. Answer her."

I turned to him quickly, fast enough to mouth, "I love you." Since then, he's played my dad in other projects, on an episode of *Beverly Hills 90210* and in the stage play *Whatever She Wants*. I always refer to him as Mr. Richard Roundtree because I love him so much. He taught me a lesson that I bring to every set: Be ready to stand up for others. I always try to be welcoming to other actors that I work with. I am never the standoffish star to the up-and-comers. It's about grace, but it's also about being smart and anticipating reversals of fortune. **Watch how you talk to people because someday they might be in the position to hire or fire you.**

I had a bigger problem than that director, and that problem's name was Jonelle Allen.

When the show first started, Jonelle was the star and she did not appreciate this new kid coming in and getting attention. I think she was kind of the set bully, and folks watched their step around her. I remember her being quite the bitch. She saw the direction the show was going with my character, and she felt I was getting a little bit big for my britches.

It blew up in hair and makeup, of course, where the real drama happens on soaps. We were each getting done up when the show publicist came in to pitch me an idea.

Jonelle snapped, "Ugh, are you guys doing another stupid magazine shoot?"

Nobody said anything, which was how I'd seen everyone react to Jonelle's outbursts. Not this time.

"Why, 'cause you're not in it?" I asked. "Again?"

And everybody in the room was like, "Oh, shit." They knew it was about to go down. If there were a microwave in there they would have been saying, "Hold up, let's make some popcorn 'cause the show is on!"

Jonelle froze. "Little girl," she said.

"Oh, I got your little girl."

She made a face, and I went in deeper. "Bitch, you picked the wrong one today."

I was ready to go twelve rounds, but Jonelle backed down. **Bullies**

come at you from a place of fear. The thing with bullies in any workplace is they don't really know how to fight and they get lazy coasting on their rep. I'm not telling you to call Jeanine the middle manager a bitch, but stand up for yourself. Jonelle was pissing on her territory because she feared losing it. If she could intimidate me into submission, she would. I offered her the opportunity to be equals, nothing less.

She grew to respect me, probably because I stood up to her, and we became friends on the set. Thank God, because one day our characters, Maya and Doreen, had to throw down in a catfight that has become legendary.

Picture young me as Maya in a skintight red glamour gown, showing up at Doreen's ivory-hued apartment to confront her about trying to get with my dad. Jonelle had a shiny yellow Alexis Carrington dress with a train. It was the makeup room all over again, only this time we had ball gowns and the campiest lines imaginable.

"What do you want?" Jonelle, in character, hissed at me.

"I want to wipe this floor with you," I said.

Well, Jonelle proceeds to throw off her fur, toss her bag, kick off her heels one by one, and lasso that train between her legs to get in a sort of sumo-princess squat position. It was all I could do not to laugh.

I kicked off my shoes, too, moved aside an armchair, and we took off our dangly earrings like ladylike prizefighters. The script had her getting the upper hand at first, but my Maya gave her all. I ripped off that train. Oh, and all hell broke loose. We trashed that set—no vase was safe from us.

The scene became legendary, and people are still talking about it. After a particularly vicious catfight on *Empire*, the next day many sites called it an homage to my *Generations* battle. Then all my friends started emailing me a YouTube video. The subject line was generally "OMG!!!" Two men had painstakingly re-created the catfight shot for shot, delivering every line and blow to perfection. I was so touched and I laughed and laughed. Now, you know I value, respect, and cherish my gay fans. But I have never loved them more.

Around this *Generations* time, I had a dear friend come out to me. Well, I made him come out to me. He spent a lot of time talking about women around me, and I could tell he was just trying to prove something to me that was false. And I didn't want that for him.

"Okay, sit your ass down." I said. "I need you to stop trying to act like you like girls. You're gay. Aren't you?"

"I am," he said. His whole body exhaled. He hadn't told anybody. Can you imagine not telling a single soul who you are? He grew up in the Bible Belt, and thought he had no choice. "Are you going to think I'm a bad person?"

"Absolutely not," I said, crying that he even thought that. "I have no right to tell you who to love. You know what I have a right to tell you: to be happy. Because I love you, and I want you to only do stuff that's gonna make you happy."

Everyone needs to be told they're great and deserving of love. God knows I do. As I was writing this book, something I said in a radio interview about *Vivica's Black Magic* was seen as homophobic. I was asked if my guys danced for men. I said no, that this was the ultimate girls' night out. I was thinking of my girls, and was also overly defensive of my guys, who have been called gay on social media by insecure people jealous of the attention these dancers get. I phrased it badly, and it turned into a headline. I didn't get much sleep for a few nights because I was trying so hard to apologize. If you need to hear it again, let me tell you now: I love you.

Once I started making a little money, I had one big wish.

"Mom, I really want you to come out here," I said. It had become a constant plea on our weekly calls. I wanted Everlyena Fox to see the mountains with her own eyes. I knew I couldn't get her to dip a toe in the ocean, but I at least wanted her to see its beauty.

Finally, she relented and came to visit me. I picked her up at the airport and gave her the biggest hug. There was so much I wanted her to see.

"You wait here," I said. "I'll bring the car."

When I drove up in my ride, she about got back on that plane. "What kind of car are *you* driving?" she said.

It was a burgundy Jeep with chrome wheels, my absolute pride and joy. God, I loved that car. The Jeep sat up a little high, and Mom kept alternating holding her seat and the door as we drove.

"I want to show you something before we go to my place," I said. I had it all planned out. I drove her up Beachwood Canyon in the Hollywood Hills, just to where you could see the Hollywood sign. It's a windy, twisty road up, and as we got higher, she kept asking how much farther it was.

"Just a little ways," I said, heading up the canyon. I kept thinking how fabulous she would think this was.

Well, she had never been so high before, and started to become terrified. "Angie, you turn this damn car around right now!" That only made Adventurous Angie try to get there faster, which, well, only made her yell louder.

When we finally stopped, she turned and hissed at me, "Girl, if you don't take my ass down from up here right quick . . ."

I did. She didn't like the race down the mountain either. I should have checked with her. But she liked my place, and that it was clean. I took her out to eat at some of my favorite places. There was one moment when we were just starting lunch, when we held hands across the table to say grace. As she spoke, I peeked up to see the California light falling on my Indiana mom, a palm tree swaying behind her. She looked beautiful. *We made it to Hollywood*, I thought.

After we said our amens, I had to ask her something. "Are you proud of me, Mom?" I asked. "I'm working."

"I like that you're being responsible and keeping your home so neat, Angie," she said. "You were always neat."

I understand now that this was the highest praise she was able to give me at the time. But back then, I just wanted her to tell me she was proud.

Generations was great for me, but as my story line built up, I was only working three days a week. That left plenty of time for me to keep my waitressing job. Yes, I kept my day job! I'd started working at the L.A. Pasta and Pizza in the Beverly Center, L.A.'s fancy mall. I was sort of half in, half out as a working actress.

One day, in the middle of a shift at the L.A. Pasta and Pizza, I brought the check to a nice couple sitting at a two-top.

"Can I ask you a question?" the woman asked me.

"Of course."

She paused. "Aren't you on a soap opera?"

"Yes," I said, still in my accommodating waitress voice, like I was saying we had a booth ready. "Generations."

"You play Maya, right?"

I couldn't hold it back. "*Yeah!*" I said. I was so touched to be recognized.

"I thought that was you!" she said. "I love you!"

"I love you back!" I said. And I did.

That was the defining moment. I was like, *Okay, if you're gonna do this acting thing, you've gotta commit.* **Yes, keep your day job, but be ready to commit to your 24-7 dream job.**

As soon as Generations upped me to four and five days a week, I quit L.A. Pasta and Pizza. Then, wouldn't you know, Generations got canceled! But I didn't regret my decision, mainly because I had $25,000 in the bank and I thought I was rich. I was sitting like a fat cat on that pile of FU money. But that money started saying, "See you," right quick. I was burning through it, auditioning again and wondering if I'd made a mistake leaving waitressing.

I turned to a friend for advice. (See, that squad comes in handy!) While doing *Generations*, I'd met a wonderful actress by the name of Sheila Wills. She'd done a lot of work in soaps and she became a real mentor to me. In fact, she is my acting coach to this day. I told her how frustrated I was getting.

"Vivica, stay ready," she told me.

For an actress, she told me, working or not, I had to take care of myself, stay in shape, and keep my skills sharp.

"When it's your turn," Sheila said, "if you are not ready and you miss out on that job that could change your life, the only person you have to blame is yourself. Your turn will be coming. Stay ready."

I treated auditions like learning experiences, meeting people and experimenting with different types of dialogue. I did stand-in work to get a sense of different sets. I didn't let anything slide.

Then I got *The Young and the Restless*. Playing sweet Dr. Stephanie Simmons seemed like winning a prize. And I got to kiss Shemar Moore, who back then was all that and a bag of chips with a helping of hot sauce.

So why wasn't I happy? I wanted more. I didn't know it at the time, but *The Young and the Restless* turned out to be my golden ticket to becoming a movie star.

KNOCK ON SUCCESS'S DOOR, HONEY. HELL, KICK IT IN.

have learned that real empowerment, for women and men, is taking charge of your life and becoming your own boss. And in building careers, some people say good things happen to those who wait. Not me. I believe good things come to those who go out and make it happen. Success won't come knocking on your door. **Knock on success's door, honey. Hell, kick it in.**

That's what I did on a morning in 1994, when I marched into my agent's office with one goal. All the black girls in Hollywood were talking about it. *Everyone* was going out to get *Independence Day*. There was a role for a kick-ass black woman in this film: Jasmine Dubrow, a love interest for Will Smith, who I liked so much from when I did an episode of *Fresh Prince*.

"How come I'm not getting an audition for *Independence Day?*" I asked.

"Aw, baby, you're on a soap opera," she said. "You know you ain't got a big enough name for that. That's a big ol' movie."

I nodded, but I didn't accept it. She was telling me to know my place: "Go on back there and learn your lines." I liked working on *The Young and the Restless*, being allowed to come into people's homes and entertain people who wanted a little escape. But I had a little voice telling me I needed to go take my career to the next level.

It turned out the wife of an *Independence Day* producer, Bill Fay, was one of those fans watching me at home. Jody Fay was laid up at home, pregnant, watching me play Dr. Simmons on *The Young and the Restless*. She called her husband. "Are you still having trouble casting Jasmine?" she asked him.

He told her that no one was sticking, and she said, "You really should try this girl."

My agent called me that day, sounding pretty amused. "The *Independence Day* casting folks called," she said, "looking for you."

I thought she was teasing me. "They called looking for *me*?" I said. "You're kidding."

"Nope," she said. "Now go on out there and go get it."

It was one of those moments where you realize your life is about to get a turbocharge. I distinctly remember hanging up the phone and saying aloud, "Here it comes."

Now, Jasmine is a stripper in the film. So, honey, I went out and got me a patent-leather white jumpsuit and killer heels. I went into that audition with my stripper gear on, and I thought I was just too fine.

The casting director was Wendy Kurtzman, a kind and direct woman. I did my read-through and she smiled. "It's a good thing you can act, dear," Wendy said. "Because that outfit? No."

"But she's a stripper," I said, suddenly feeling much, much less than too fine.

"Dear, she's a stripper with a heart of gold," she said, no-nonsense.

"She strips for a *living*. Now, I want you to watch the movie *Speed* and study Sandra Bullock. *That* kind of look. You have to have *that* kind of feel to you. You can audition again."

I am so glad I stayed present and took the note not as criticism but as insight. She wanted me to succeed, and her comments were the tools I needed to do better. You can't swat away advice like that. Take it, consider it, and decide if it's something you need to hear.

So I did my homework. I rented *Speed* that night and I was like, *Oh, I get it now.* And when I went back in to audition, I wore a cute summer dress and I'd got me some little combat boots and ankle socks with lace on them.

As soon as I walked in, Wendy said, "There you go. Now you understand."

I had the look, but I still needed to get the role. In total, I had to audition six times. Finally, they called me and said, "Vivica, you got the part." I ran around my house screaming. They'd been stuck so long on Jasmine they needed me the very next day. It was like, boom, I'm racing around in a truck and jumping over stuff. They thrust me right in there.

But I'd prepared. I knew every line and was ready. There were no excuses. And it's a good thing, because the director, Roland Emmerich, told me a secret at the *Independence Day* premiere. "Did you know," he asked in his cute German accent, "that if you didn't do good your first day of filming, that we were going to fire you?"

"Really?"

"Yeah, because there was one girl that was our first choice, Kristen Wilson," Roland said. "But she was doing a show with Montel Williams so she was unavailable. Your first day of filming they called and said, 'Okay, we'll work with your schedule. She's available now.'"

Roland laughed at my look of shock. He'd clearly been sitting on this one for a while. He said he and the producers immediately looked at my dailies. "Nope," he remembered them all saying, "she's right for Jasmine."

My entire career was on the line that first day on the set, and I had no idea. You've got to show up and be present, because you never know who is watching you and deciding if you need a promotion or a job. When you are doing the work you love, not calling it in on some job you're coasting in, you need to be on it every single day. That's what makes a boss.

Meanwhile, during filming, I thought the biggest pressure on me was my stripping scene. You know I took that seriously. I even got a stripper tutor. They found a local strip joint, and I met a stripper there at nine o'clock in the morning when the place was closed. We had "class" every morning for a week, and sister was strict. Like she was doing freaking Juilliard for strippers.

She gave me the ground rules the first day.

"I want you to lose your inhibitions," she said. "I want you to come in from now on in four-inch heels. You can have shorts on, but I want you to wear a G-string underneath."

"Okay," I said, in the meekest little church-girl voice in the world.

But I did it. Next time we met, she was still all business. "Take off the shorts and walk around," she said. "Let's get you comfortable parading around."

"All right," I said back. **"Time to get comfortable being uncomfortable."**

She turned out to be the perfect teacher for me. By the time we were filming they had this big bikini bottom thing ready for me to put on, and I was like, "Nope, I'm committed. G-string." She had made me so comfortable that I didn't even realize I would be on film walking in all ass out. At the premiere, I won't lie, I was like, *Whoa.* My mom was shocked. "You had your butt out there for all to see!" she said. But at least it's nice and tight.

I also had a personal trainer named Will Smith. Yes, *that* one. Lord, he did not give me a break. We were filming in Wendover, Utah, which we all called Bendover, Utah, 'cause it was such a small town that there was fuck all to do there. We were there two weeks, and early on I had a couple of days off. They'd put us all up in this big house, and I was hanging out by the Jacuzzi, having a margarita. What else was there to do?

Then Will walked by and did a double take.

"What are you doing?" he said, as serious as a heart attack.

"Um, having a drink? It's my day off."

"Vivica, come here," he said. "We are going upstairs and we are gonna do push-ups and do weights. You have to realize this movie is going to be big. This movie is going to change our lives—it's important for us to show up and be good."

I put down the margarita. He was a tough taskmaster, but he was right. When you have the gift of an opportunity in your career, do everything you can to make the most of it. **Don't let someone else work harder than you, because you will be handing them the keys to your dream.**

And yes, it was a big deal that here we were making a movie about two black people and a Jewish guy who save the world. I would talk to Will about what that could mean for the African American community, but he saw it as a bigger thing.

"I don't want you to think of it that way," I recall him telling me. "You just have to be a strong woman. Somebody that they don't look at based on your skin color."

I got that. You know that I am black and I'm proud. But I don't want to be seen solely for my color. People don't say Meryl Streep or Jennifer Lawrence are wonderful white actresses, and I will leave it at that.

Will was dating Jada Pinkett, who I thought was just fantastic.

They met when she auditioned for *Fresh Prince of Bel-Air*, but they thought she was too short! Nia Long got the gig instead. So I had to tell Jada, "Listen, I have to kiss your man in this movie." She gave me her blessing and told me to go for it. "Just bring the Binaca."

Our big kissing scene was shot outside at night. It was bone-ass cold and we were crying from the wind in our eyes. I didn't have to warn Jada because it was the furthest thing from sexy! We'd kiss kiss kiss, wipe the snot away, spray the Binaca. Kiss kiss kiss, wipe the snot away, spray the Binaca. We ended up winning Best Kiss at the MTV Movie Awards.

Will also helped me plan the next step in my career, *Set It Off*. The director, F. Gary Gray, was friends with Will and came to visit the *Independence Day* set. Jada Pinkett had already been cast, and I'd grown so close to Will and Jada that Gary saw me coming on the film as a family thing. He was so young, twenty-five, and wanted to make sure he worked with people he liked. He said to me, "Yo, I've got this movie . . ."

He told me he wanted me for Frankie, the bank teller who gets fired from her job after having a gun held to her head during a robbery. She grew up in the projects with the robber, and so the bank wrongly accuses her of being in collusion. Fed up, she begins robbing banks with three girlfriends. "But the studio wants Rosie Perez for Frankie." My face fell. Rosie was so talented, and had been nominated for an Oscar for *Fearless*. He asked if I could audition for T.T., the sweet new mom, but also come in ready to read for Frankie.

Will had read Jada's script, and as soon as I told him about the double audition, he was clear about my game plan.

"You can do T.T., but you really gotta get Frankie," he said. "You gotta go in there and take that shit. **Take what should be yours.**"

He started slamming his fist in his hand like a motivational speaker—which, in that moment, he was. He knew Frankie's story was the biggest in the film because she was who the viewer would identify with as she responds to having her back against the wall. And he also knew people saw me as just the pretty girl. A glamour girl is limited because she doesn't get to do the gritty parts. They didn't know I was Angie Fox who grew up by the projects.

"You gotta go in there and be pretty and be a bank teller and be professional," he said. "But when they do you wrong, you gotta bring it, V. Your main note is that you want revenge."

I auditioned on a lunch break, and I got the part. Gary told me when I said Frankie's lines, he was like, "Where did Vivica go?" I will always love Will for coaching me to be my best.

I got to bond with those ladies on the film: Queen Latifah (who still calls me Big V), Jada, and Kimberly Elise. We rehearsed and rehearsed, and became as tight as our characters were in the film. To make our friendship believable on-screen, Gary wanted us to hang out and chill off the set. Do the things that our characters do together so that we had an ease and history with each other that would translate to the screen.

We were all nuts about one another right away. Kimberly was from the theater and was so quiet but so talented. She had a young child of her own, so the main ones who hung out all the time were me, Jada, and Latifah. The funny thing is that Jada was such a hip-hop head as a teenager in Baltimore that she worked in a club where Latifah did an appearance. Jada hadn't even heard her music yet, but was so hungry for female role models that when she saw a photo of Latifah, she demanded that she be the emcee and introduce Latifah that night. Meanwhile, Latifah was so young she had her mom with her! Two kindred spirits recognizing that drive early.

I introduced Latifah to sushi when we were downtown and the only place that was open was a sushi spot.

"Girl, I'm from the East Coast," she told me flat-out, putting on her Newark accent as thick as possible. "We don't be eatin' no raw stuff."

"Girl, you don't have to eat everything that's raw," I said, coming back at her full Indy. "I got you."

"If I am paying for that food, they'd better cook it."

Sure enough, she loved it. "Wow, this is good!" she said. To this day when we meet up for a meal, we have sushi to commemorate our start.

As I got closer to Jada, I had a front row seat to watching Will court her. Will approached it like he did everything that was important to him. He was not playing and was putting it down. Every week during the course of *Set It Off*, there was an escalation. First it was a thousand roses in her dressing room. Then it was a marquise diamond necklace. By the end it was a convertible Mercedes. He was saying to her and to everyone around, "You are the one. You are the one."

I can't talk about Jada without paying tribute to her as a mother. I watched how having those two gorgeous, interesting, smart children, Willow and Jaden, transformed her. She became regal. When she speaks to those kids, she reminds me of my teacher Mrs. Fletcher, the one who would see every conversation as an opportunity to teach and learn.

The biggest lesson Jada gave me was when I was rushing through lines on the set. I had gotten used to soap acting, where time is everything and you have to just get it done. We were rehearsing, and a scene just wasn't gelling for me.

"Do you realize why you're not getting what you want?" she asked me.

I hadn't thought of it that way. I was just plowing through, saying the lines.

"**Take your moment**," she said. "Let that emotion happen for you, V."

She was right. I still do that now. I do a lot of work to get into character before the camera starts rolling or I walk out onstage. I create backstory and develop mannerisms. If my character has a certain job—whether I'm playing a beauty blogger or the President of the United States—I am all over YouTube watching videos of people who do that, to get the cadence of how they speak and the carriage of their bodies. All that preparation creates the bones of the character, but I still have to breathe life into it. Take my moment, let the emotion come in so I can feel it and be authentic as I tell the story.

Gary was one of the best directors I've ever worked with. He had a strong, clear vision of what he wanted and demanded excellence. One time during filming we all went to lunch and came back, I swear, two minutes late. Gary let us have it.

"Y'all late," he said.

I care about being on time. It's one of my things. Still, I said, "We're hardly late."

"Y'all got to understand I'm serious about this movie," said Gary. "People gonna come to the theater thinking they are gonna laugh at y'all women. We gotta make it work. We are making a classic."

He was tough, but the thing that made him so great as a director and as a boss was that he would bend if the idea merited it. I had ad-libbed a line during my audition, and it wasn't in the script when it came time to shooting. It was when Frankie, shell-shocked from the robbery, is interrogated by the police about knowing the robber. Meanwhile, she is covered in blood from seeing a woman get shot in the head. The script said there were two detectives, one a black woman and the other a white man who does all the talking. I thought, even though it's the police, there has to be one woman-to-woman moment there. As Frankie leaves, trying to hold her head high,

I paused to say to the black detective, played by Ella Joyce, "You didn't bother to ask me if I was thirsty, sister."

It didn't make it into the shooting script, and I asked Gary if I could try the line for the film.

"Give me one," I said, "Can you give me just one?"

That's the thing. Give a director or boss what they think they need, and then you can say, "Hey, can I have this take for me?" If you show up prepared, knowing your lines and allowing everyone to work efficiently, that structure you have helped create gives you freedom. Once you give them what they need, you allow them the opportunity to say, "Sure, go for it." We did the second take, and that's the one he used. He told me that when he saw it in the editing room, he threw his hands up and yelled, "This child right there!"

The dumbest thing to do is to walk in new and just say, "I know what will work." Turnoff number one: "I know better."

The last six of the nine weeks of shooting were filmed at night. I decided we had all become vampires. It took a bit for our sleep schedules to get back on track, but it was so worth it. *Set It Off* helped me show that I wasn't only a glamour girl standing next to the hero: "I'll wait here while you save me!" You see Frankie make a transition when the chips are down, becoming completely hood while maintaining her strength and her integrity. I'll never forget running into Dominique Wilkins during All-Star Weekend after *Set It Off* came out. Here was this basketball legend—without question one of the greatest dunkers in NBA history—running up to me.

"Vivica!"

"What's up, 'Nique?"

"Vivica, *Set It Off*!"

"What about it?"

"Yo, I had to go see that shit two days in a row!" he said. "I was crying. That movie was good as hell."

I still have grown men coming up to me saying that Frankie made them cry. That year was a lesson in diversifying. *Independence Day* had an $80 million budget and a huge marketing campaign. *Set It Off* had $9 million and word of mouth. I am so proud that all of those actresses are still doing incredible work today, and that Gary went on to be handed the keys to the *Fast and the Furious* megafranchise.

Set It Off showed my different strengths. I have said time and again that for me, my versatility has equaled my longevity. **You can't get typecast in life.** If I stayed the glamour girl, who was going to hire me when Hollywood said I was too old for those roles? There is a shelf life for certain chapters in your life, especially in entertainment. If you learn how to go into each chapter gracefully, then you can extend the longevity of your career. Because so many people hold on to being the young hot chick, and you're like, "Girl, let it go. You no longer can do that." You need a second act. I ask them what I ask myself: "What you got next, bitch?"

So what have you got to keep you from getting typecast in life? How are you diversifying? Let's go through some quicksand scenarios that might be keeping you from moving forward and reaching your real goals.

1. Your job won't let you grow.

People get used to seeing you in a certain way and those perceptions get stuck. And then you—and your career—get stuck. If you're Judy in accounting but you want to be president of the company, you need to show you can do more than what's expected. "You're Judy in accounting," they might as well say in your always positive employee evaluations. "We will never promote you because what would we do if we didn't have you in Accounting?"

Ah, but if they outsourced the work and closed her department, they would certainly figure out what to do without Judy in accounting. In my world, it's why I prefer to do a movie over a television series. With TV, a studio can pull the plug on you at any moment.

Or put you on Saturday nights at nine-thirty, then say, "Hmm, ratings are down. Sorry." There's really no security. When you do a film, you've got your schedule and you've got your cast and crew. It's rare at that point that they'll say, "Everyone go home." They've invested the money, they want a return, and box office receipts don't lie.

So I would tell Judy to show that her skill set goes beyond what she is already doing. Make it clear in those evaluations that she wants a different role and can do new things. And privately, I would tell Judy to prepare to do those things elsewhere if she can't achieve her goals at her current job.

2. You've been bought.

I love money—I'm not stupid—but I love what it can do. I love the freedom it gives me to sometimes take risks, but mostly I love how it enables me to take parts I want. On some sets the routine is, "May I bring a café mocha to your trailer, Ms. Fox?" Other movies are, "Coffee's over there, I think there's some left." I do a cost-benefit analysis. If it's work that I will wake up excited to do or that will open up bigger opportunities for me in acting, it is worth the investment of my time.

What is your cost-benefit analysis? Does your job pay so much simply because it sucks? Are you on your phone 24-7? Thinking about work with dread when you're trying to sleep? Or answering emails when you're at the playground with your kid? Times have changed, and I know that's a reality for many people in the work-force, but if all that effort is just making your boss super rich and you kind of, sort of rich, then you should examine that. If you worked out the by-the-minute charges, perhaps you would be happier mak-ing less money but having more time for yourself. Or working just as hard, even harder, on something that was yours.

I know the pressures of being a provider. But it's your life and your dreams. Talk to the people you're supporting, especially your spouse, and tell them how much more you could be for them if you were working toward a real goal. Enlist them in the enterprise. Otherwise you might resent them for making you work at a job you hate, and they will have no idea they're the reason.

3. You're afraid to try.

You are comfortable in the chair you're in. Nobody else is after it, I bet. You can practically do what you do in your sleep, day in, day out. Perhaps you mentor young people at your job, then watch them rise in the ranks—past you—while you keep doing what you're doing. You're pulling a paycheck, you eat at your desk, you're fine . . . but you're not. If you're not in love with your job, you are going through the motions.

I did stand-in work when I was starting out. That means you literally stand in for a busier actress that you resemble so they can light you, block out the scene, and have it all ready for the real star. I did that for Jasmine Guy when she was guesting on *Fresh Prince*. I could have settled for that and had fun stories from a studio set. But I wanted to be the real star.

Just as I kept auditioning, I advise you to keep your interviewing skills sharp by going out for new jobs. Devote one day to your résumé. Screw laundry, sorry. It will be there. Just do it and have a trusted friend look at it because you want to get it right. It's so easy these days to apply for jobs on sites like Indeed.com. The downside is that you are one of many, so you have to really bring it when you land an interview.

People don't believe me now because it is such a classic romantic comedy, but I turned down the *Two Can Play That Game* script three times. It was a battle-of-the-sexes kind of thing. My character, Shanté Smith, was the lead, and she was just such a bitch. You were supposed to root for her to win back this guy, but what you really wanted to tell him was to run away! I also felt this was a missed opportunity to show sisterhood with Shanté's girlfriends. They had to be real. Because a woman knows her girlfriends can sometimes be everything to her. This just wasn't the image I wanted to portray for my first time as the lead in a movie.

So I was straight with the writer-director, Mark Brown. "Look, until y'all write it so it's something I can be proud of, I'm cool where I'm at."

I didn't settle, because I knew it was a good idea with the potential to be great. Mark just needed to work on it. So he went back and made the characters stronger and more likable. And believable, because you have to really think that each thinks the other is worthy of compromise. Because that's what true love is. Each person deep down thinks they're getting the better end of the deal, right?

In the end, Shanté became much more real, a lot like me, in fact. She's an advertising exec who is sophisticated, but she can still be your girl from around the way. What I loved about the film was that it showed a side of the African American community that was not seen on-screen at the time: the upper-middle-class brothers and sisters who like the finer things. If a brother or sister had money in movies back then, he was a drug kingpin or it was a joke: Isn't it weird that this black person has money? Not this movie. Shanté lives in a beautiful home, dresses to the nines, and drives a convertible Jaguar. As Shanté puts it: "If you haven't noticed, I'm a sister. An educated, strong sister who remembers where she came from—and knows where she's going." It said to the audience, "Yes, this exists, and yes, this is possible for you, too." And frankly, it helped the brand of Vivica Fox. You saw a beautifully dressed woman who works hard, and you wanted to hang out with her.

I had such a vision of Shanté that me and the woman in Wardrobe sometimes had, uh, disagreements. My outfit in the opening scene was crucial. It had to be killer, because there's a long walk through Shanté's office that establishes her power in the firm, and also shows men reacting to my . . . assets. I take a springtime drive, and when I get out of the car, I have to keep the viewer's eye as I do a monologue about her life and men. I wanted to just pop on the screen, and if I had to pay for the outfit myself, I had no problem getting out my brand-new AmEx.

I was out shopping with my friend Cassandra Mills, this gorgeous entertainment executive, and I was telling her about the scene.

"What color is the car?" she asked.

"A dark red," I said.

"Think yellow," she said.

"Like ketchup and mustard," I said. Of course. A classic contrast. Armed with my AmEx, she and I went on a hunt. We found this Easter-yellow Versace power pantsuit that was just slamming when I tried it on.

"Get that tailored," she said. "Bring it in on the booty and that'll be the one."

"Charge it!" I yelled.

Once it fit like a second skin, the suit completely made the scene. Style is a weapon in Shanté's arsenal, so I had to make sure it was perfection.

Morris Chestnut defined perfection as Shanté's love interest and opponent, Keith. Lord, I knew Morris from our *Out All Night* days. He was a kid then, playing video games, nobody's hunk, but now he was this man. When we had kissing scenes, that was the only time that I ever lost myself in kissing another actor. He was that good. I damn near forgot the cameras were rolling. Hands down, the best kisser I have ever had on-screen. But don't worry, you know Vivica always keeps things professional. I like to tell people, "I kissed Morris Chestnut for all the ladies!"

I still had one problem with the script, and I was really irritated about it. Shanté constantly breaks the fourth wall, talking to the audience and giving the real skinny on what's actually happening beneath the dialogue. I pictured the audience screaming at me, "Turn around and act, bitch! Stop talking so much. Do you know you're in a movie?" I kept mentioning this to Mark, who was really good about listening to me. Finally a producer on the film had enough.

"Vivica, just go rent *Ferris Bueller's Day Off*," he said. "He does it really well."

I listened and did my homework, thank God. Watching Matthew Broderick was a revelation. The voice didn't have to be all-knowing, but conspiratorial and just honest. From my first words to the viewer, an "Oh, hey," like you just walked into the scene and I need to catch you up, we are best friends. After watching *Ferris*, I apologized for not understanding earlier. "I got it now," I said. **When you receive constructive criticism and it helps you deliver, you have to acknowledge it.**

I loved my girls in that movie, Tamala Jones, Wendy Raquel Robinson, and Mo'Nique. Mo'Nique was a wonder, let me tell you. She was one of the last people cast, playing my fashionista friend. The role was originally supposed to be Tyra Banks, and Mo'Nique just loved that she was this big, beautiful woman who was completely believable as my most fashionable friend. She told me her agent called her on a Friday and said, "There's a Vivica Fox movie starting Monday, are you in?" She said yes without reading the script, and she is so funny in the film.

She had a gift for making the friendship seem real on-screen. There's a party scene where Morris is dancing up on some women, trying to make me jealous. The three girls are like a Greek chorus, with this rising crescendo of each saying, "What you gon' do, Shanté?"

Well, she improvised, "What you gon' do, bitch?"

Mark, the director, jumped in. "No, no, no," he said. "They're friends. She can't call you 'bitch.'"

There was a pause and I just took him aside.

"Mark, that's Shanté's girl," I said. "She sure can call me 'bitch.' This is really how girls speak to each other when it's just them. It's like a term of affection."

There was someone who always called me "bitch" around that time, and I loved her for it. Ms. Whitney Houston. Her then-husband, Bobby Brown, had landed a small role in *Two Can Play That Game*. Whitney called me just before shooting started.

"Bitch, you better look out for my boy," she said.

"You know it," I said. "I got you."

We connected because our images in magazines were like ice princesses. Black Barbies. But we knew the truth: She had that Jersey in her, and I grew up two blocks from the projects. So we could hang. One night after filming, she called me.

"Hey, what are you doing?" she said. "You want to go out?"

"Girl, I'm just in a warm-up suit."

"Oh, don't worry, I'm casual, too."

So we decided to meet at the Hotel Bel-Air. As my friend Darren Bond and I were pulling up, there was Whitney. She was wearing an $850,000 sable-fur full-length coat. A star of old Hollywood ready for her close-up.

"Casual?" I yelled. "Casual?"

"Oh, this?" She laughed that huge, amazing laugh of hers and threw the fur on a chair. "I got my jeans on!"

We had some drinks at the bar and got someone to round up a deck of cards. Then we headed to her room and played spades for hours. As we talked, we of course got to what music we loved. We started doing Sade songs together like "No Ordinary Love" and "Smooth Operator." Whitney was a human being who wanted to live, to love, and to have that private time. To sing just for herself, and not always be a singing doll in a little glass case. When it becomes boring and too much pressure, people rebel. You're like, *I don't want to be perfect today.*

I have a portrait of her in my bedroom that I wake up to every day. And she is smiling, because that's how I want to remember her.

Two Can Play That Game opened September 7, 2001. We premiered at the old Cineplex Odeon in Century City, and I got out of the limo and saw "Starring Vivica A. Fox" on the marquee. It was the best feeling in the world. The movie made more than its budget back in the first weekend, and I was set to go on *The Tonight Show with Jay Leno* that Tuesday.

Then of course 9/11 happened and there were more important things to worry about. But people are still discovering the film because Mark put in that effort to make it great. When a girl comes up to me with a big, knowing smile, I know she is either going to be telling me all about *Two Can Play That Game*—or my wigs!

They told me I had fifteen minutes with Quentin Tarantino.

"Quentin's going to meet with you in a coffee shop," my agent said.

"A coffee shop?"

"It's to see whether or not he likes you," she said. "Then he'll let you know if he wants to see you for the part."

I thought, *That's some shit, but okay.* He'd written a role for a black woman in *Kill Bill*, a script that was already getting so much buzz. Vernita Green was a cold-blooded assassin hiding out in the suburbs of Pasadena—until Uma Thurman comes to get hers.

I was so anxious when I got to that coffee shop. It was like an audition for an audition. The first thing he told me was that he was in a video store and saw my name on the cover of the *Two Can Play That Game* DVD.

"I was like, 'Vivica Fox!'" he said, shouting my name like I already was an action hero. "I am going to take this home, and if she moves me on the screen, that's who's gonna play my Vernita Green."

Quentin loves telling stories, and if he likes you, oh, he is going to talk. At like Mach 5. We discussed favorite movies, of course. I talked about Pam Grier and how much I loved her, and Richard Roundtree, who'd played my dad on *Generations*. "Yeah, I'm Shaft's daughter," I joked.

The fifteen-minute meeting stretched to an hour and a half, until he said, "I'm going to send you a scene and I'm going to come to your house and we'll work through it together."

"My house?"

"Yeah."

"Promise me you won't hold my house against me?"

"What are you talking about?"

"Just promise me, Quentin."

He did, and I'm sure he suspected I was a hoarder or some crazy person living in a tiny house. The truth was that I was living in a huge eight-thousand-square-foot mansion in Tarzana. I'd invested in real estate, was doing very well, thank you, and this place frankly looked like a diva lived there. It was straight out of *Dynasty*, with a double staircase and huge chandelier right when you walked in.

It could easily be mistaken for the home of a spoiled brat who would never follow direction. This was a time in film when studios were not playing. They were tired of problem actors and had dealt with their spoiled stars shutting down productions because of heroin problems. They wanted workers on the straight and narrow, and any red flags could put me out of the running.

I was afraid he would take one look at the place and say, "Here I thought Vivica was hungry." I still was.

So when I answered the door, his greeting was: "Holy shit, this is your house."

"You promised me you wouldn't hold it against me."

"Holy shit," he said again. "I'm not. Let me see this place."

Before I could say anything, he helped himself to a tour like he was scouting a location. When he was done, he said he wanted to do the scene in the kitchen. Just like in the film.

He made me read it twice. And then, like he was making an idle remark, he said, "Very good. You are my Vernita Green. I'm hungry, do you want sushi?"

We went out to Kushiyu on Ventura in Tarzana. At dinner, he told me his plan for the film: There would be no quick cuts or getting away with special effects to make us look like real warriors. I had to commit to six months of training, and all of the actors needed to become experts in martial arts to make his vision real on the screen.

"No problem," I said, thinking back to my high school athlete days. Piece of cake.

Ha.

For three months, Uma Thurman, Lucy Liu, Daryl Hannah, David Carradine, and I spent eight hours a day studying martial arts at a gym they put together in Culver City. It was nine to five, Monday through Friday. If you didn't walk in the door between 8:55 and 8:59, you were in trouble at 9:01. I thought I was in the damn Olympics or something.

Uma was three months out from having her gorgeous baby boy, Roan, and she also brought her equally beautiful four-year-old, Maya, along. Of all the girls on set, I think Uma liked me best because of her kids. I used to play with them all the time. That baby boy would stare into my eyes. "Vivica," she said one day, "I think he's in love." She and I were on strict diets, and we had a ritual of spending our one cheat day a week hanging out at this bowling alley Maya loved. We'd eat slice after slice of cheap pizza, loving every bit of it.

At first, Uma was frustrated because all the other women on the film were dropping weight so quickly with the intense training. I mean, the woman had just had a child. "Don't worry," I said, "it'll come off." She went to Tokyo to film for a month, and when I saw her again, I walked right past her. She yelled, "Yay! I got skinny!"

Uma needed all the support she could get—the movie rested on her shoulders. She was so busy, and then her and Daryl had that blonde competition thing going on. And I was like, *I'm gonna be cool with you and I'm gonna be cool with everybody. I'm not in a pissing contest.*

I have to tell you—whether you're on a movie set or working at a law firm, some people will try to pull you into their drama and make you pick sides. Don't fall for it. **Think for yourself and stay above the fray.**

Drama aside, the training itself was brutal. We'd do fight choreography, knife throwing, samurai lessons, and hit the treadmill and weights in between. They liked me because I could do them high kicks from being a cheerleader. And every Friday, at the end of the day, Quentin would gather us around and give us a review. He called it his "State of the Union." We all had to sit and listen.

The first week Quentin cut into us, telling us we had to work harder. Okay, I can work harder.

Second week, we got the same thing after we busted our asses. He said we weren't giving it our all.

Third Friday, I was so proud of all that our team had accomplished. I was sitting between cute little Lucy and sweet Uma, and I was ready for a high five for all of us.

Instead, Quentin tore into us. Something about us lollygagging in the morning, taking too long to suit up and gabbing over coffee. He said we should get here at eight-thirty, a half hour early, if we wanted to do all that.

I raised my hand. "Hold up."

And I lost it on him. "Is this a 'beat us up' contest?" I asked. "Are we fucking doing anything right? Goddamn." Everyone gasped. I felt Uma draw back. Lucy grabbed my hand and was trying to do a kind of acupressure on me, whispering, "Calm down. Calm down."

I couldn't. I kept sputtering, thinking I was taking a stand for everyone. And finally Quentin sort of said he appreciated the work but he wanted us all to do our best and to trust him.

Uma came up to me after. "Come here," she said. She put her arm on my shoulder and those beautiful eyes of hers locked on mine.

"You know, Uma, it's bullshit," I said.

She repeated in her calm, meditative voice, "I've worked with him. I've worked with him. I've worked with him. And . . . it's how he does things. He doesn't mean anything by it, it's just how he gets down."

"Well, God," I sputtered, "I mean, we're working our fucking asses off. And it's like, you know, we're not doing anything right."

"What you need to do is learn how to manipulate the situation better. Then you can get what you want."

I was all righteous. "I don't have to *manipulate* nobody," I said. "That's not me. I don't have to kiss his ass."

She cocked her head. "No, I don't mean like that," she said, still speaking in that calm, soothing voice. "You have to learn to be quiet, speak less. He's tough, but he's not stupid. He'll concede you something if it's to make the film better. Learn to attack intelligently, Vivica. Because he's got the power to fire you."

And she told me she didn't want that to happen. "But thank you for speaking up," she said.

That moment was pure sisterhood. She was honestly looking out for me. She wanted me to advocate for myself, but to do it in a way that was more constructive. I'll admit, it still took me a minute to figure out what she was talking about.

I was driving home from Culver City when I realized why she had touched me so deeply. I thought about my dad, and when he would tell me not to just go off on the basketball court when all my energy had me spazzing out. "*Attack intelligently,*" he would tell me, the exact same words Uma used. "Don't blow it by blowing up."

When it came time for real rehearsals and filming, I got to see Uma give a master class in being a movie star and leader on the set.

I watched her argue with Quentin, intelligently and successfully, for wardrobe changes and even dialogue rewrites. She made it a true collaboration, pushing him away from simply making an ode to the samurai films he made us all watch with him, toward something *new*. *Kill Bill* is an astonishing work because of their shared efforts, and it's because they each approached it not as a job, but as a cornerstone of their careers.

I know it's the work that I am most proud of in *my* career. It took four days to film our fight scene, and on the last day I took a long bath when it was over. I sat in the tub and counted all the bruises on my arms and legs. I got up to thirty. And I did so with gratitude. I was proud of my battle scars. I had done a Tarantino film, and nobody could take that accomplishment from me. Quentin is a fabulous director and I'd love to work with him again. I appreciate those endless hours in the Culver City torture chamber. It was his way of breaking us down to build us back up.

From Uma, I learned so much about sharing power. She wanted me to do my best. That hasn't always been the case for black actresses in film. I think the dirty secret of why African American actresses are only now getting more opportunities is that directors were afraid to put a sister against a white actress. Because they knew the sister, who'd had to work her ass off to get to that moment, was always going to shine like the brightest light and blow the white actress off the screen. I say put me with the best. Because if she's bringing her A game, I'm bringing my A-*plus* game. And we gonna turn this mother out.

PART TWO

FIND YOUR DREAM— AND ACTUALLY MAKE IT HAPPEN

YOU CAN'T AIM IF YOU DON'T HAVE A TARGET

just want to briefly address the reader who might be saying, "Shoot, I don't know what my dream is." Calm down. Let's figure it out together.

I'm going to give you some exercises, and the only thing I ask is that you think big.

1. Make a list of jobs you wouldn't hate doing.

I phrase it like that because sometimes when you're unhappy with where you are in life, or facing a setback, it's hard to imagine liking work. So what wouldn't suck? Go as pie-in-the-sky or far-fetched as you want. That list will tell a lot about you. A friend of mine, Mary, had worked in the corporate litigation department of a law firm for about six years. She had been passed over for partner, and wasn't sure if she even wanted to make partner anymore. She was miserable. One day after we talked on the phone, she wrote a list of about ten jobs she wouldn't mind doing. Let's look at the pros and cons of just two from the list:

Yoga instructor
Divorce lawyer

Examining each one revealed what she truly wanted in life. Her reasoning for considering becoming a yoga instructor seemed obvious to me because she goes every week. But as she talked to me later, her reasons became more detailed. "I like helping people and making that connection," Mary said. "I would save money on classes, obviously, but there's a teaching aspect to it that I like."

As she imagined the scenario, she pictured her own studio. She didn't want to partner with an existing facility because she was tired of dealing with office politics and clearing everything with someone else. Going on her own would mean finding a space and keeping it maintained, not to mention finding the students to fill it with. She would also need to be certified as an instructor to run a yoga school. That would take two hundred hours of training and money for classes. It didn't seem like a return on her investment in law school, or the hours she spent miserable in the law firm. "I needed a return on all that time," she told me.

When she thought about starting her own private practice as a divorce lawyer, she realized it provided some of the things she liked. She would be the boss and wouldn't have to answer to anyone. She would be helping people through a crisis, teaching them how to look out for themselves. And since she was already licensed as a lawyer, there was no more certification needed other than the continuing education that all lawyers have to do to maintain their bar status.

Mary became a divorce attorney, and re-created some of the aspects she liked working in a big firm. She works in a shared work space with a host of other entrepreneurs who can book conference rooms to meet clients. She also uses an inexpensive call service to answer her phones, so that no matter what, the client feels someone is working on their case. "There are things I miss about firm life," she told me. "Like having support staff and not working so much on weekends. I'm always working now. But it's work I love."

So let's go over her pros: being her own boss, low overhead, no fee for certification—and don't forget happiness.

2. What makes you stick out?

This is usually the thing that we initially think might be an obstacle, but turns out to be an asset. Growing up I thought it was my name, because it was so uncommon. Now, people say "Vivica," and you know who they're talking about. For Mary, it was that she was a woman in a law firm. She felt barred from the boys' club. "Meetings had a funny way of continuing afterward at the urinals!" she said. "Then I'd hear, 'Oh, Bob said I should . . .'"

Now potential clients sometimes seek her out as a divorce attorney specifically *because* she is a woman. Some men want a woman to represent them in court as part of their strategy, and some women want to speak to someone they know understands them.

Another way Mary sticks out is that she is a member of the LGBT community. With same-sex marriage comes same-sex divorce. She can genuinely market herself to that community and also feel good about being a real resource to them.

3. Ask people what your strengths are.

I know it's hard, but just do it. I always tell the exceptional actors in my life, "You're used to being you." They do all these great things that no one else can do, and it's become so ho-hum that people don't mention it. It becomes so that even they lose sight of what makes them such assets to the work. This isn't fishing for compliments from coworkers and friends. It's figuring out what you're actually good at and asking for examples of why they thought that. This list of strengths will reveal what you bring to the table, and give you a script for how you present yourself in an interview or with a potential client: "I'm a closer. Put me in a room and I can use my people skills to sell an idea." "I have never missed a single deadline." "I have a levity that can calm people down in high-pressure situations."

4. Make a vision board (and tack a to-do list next to it).

Anytime you see someone or something that inspires you professionally, tear it out or print it up and put it on your vision board. This isn't an afternoon activity with an excuse to buy magazines. This is an ongoing process of finding articles and images that speak to you as a worker bee.

Next to that board, I need you to put a blank sheet of paper, and it cannot stay blank for long. That is where you will list the concrete, positive steps you are doing to get to what's on that vision board. This has to be an everyday ritual. It's paying off a bill. It's contacting one of those people on your vision board and asking to shadow them or just talk on the phone. This is about doing the work, so make sure you're doing something you love.

Since I'm asking you to think about what your dreams are, I need to tell you why acting is *my* dream job.

Last night I was in a stage play, and it reminded me why I love what I do. It was at Philadelphia's Merriam Theater. Built nearly one hundred years ago, this stage has hosted greats like Sammy Davis Jr., Katharine Hepburn, and Helen Hayes. They took the same breath I did before walking out, and maybe had the same butterflies I did. Yes, I still get butterflies—from acting and from certain men.

And there was the audience, ready to give me that immediate feedback of love. The butterflies go, and you get a warm feeling in the pit of your stomach. It really is that cliché of surprise every time. *They like me. They really, really like me.* But you gotta do the work. You gotta earn the applause. It's not just given. So hold for applause, and then deliver.

Last night was in front of a mostly black audience, and they are the best. 'Cause they let you know whether the show is working or whether it's not. Black audiences are part of the show, let me tell you. "Oh, child!" someone says. "Yes, get that bitch! Don't let that bitch in."

There was one girl last night in the front row who really stood out. I thought she was gonna climb up there to join me. During this big confrontation scene between me and the ex-wife of the lead, this pretty girl yelled, "Tell her, Vivica! Tell her ass. Oh, I can't with her. No, she ain't up there talking to *my* girl."

When things like that happen, it takes all of my training to stay in character and not give her a smile. Or just flub my line.

Forgetting your line is every actor's nightmare, but it happens to everyone. That's when you depend on your costar. There were a couple of times last night where I knew we messed up, but you can't let it derail you. It's like troubleshooting any problem in business. Keep calm, and carry on. If you kind of mess up a line, then just bring it back.

One trick that I pass on to the actors I do stage plays with is that the audience is not sitting there with the script, reading along. This is something I actually learned on *Dancing with the Stars*, of all places. I kept worrying about messing up a sequence of moves.

"They don't know the choreography," my dance partner and teacher, Nick Kosovich, told me. "They will only know you messed up if you tell them. So don't tell them." **Don't point out the slips that only you know you made.**

Doing a play is completely different from doing a film or TV show. With those there is so much waiting. You are in and out of character, constantly being stopped for touch-ups or lighting tweaks. You listen to direction and get a few tries. You do it and it's done, there on film forever. On the plus side, so many people see it and can discover it years and years later.

With a stage play it's kind of like being pregnant. You're molding this story, and opening night you give birth and hope the kid turns out to be a good kid. You gotta get in there and do the work and plant the seed and make sure that the lines work and that things are funny. I worry about wardrobe, makeup, lighting—the things that I normally don't have to worry about when I do TV. There my job is to learn my lines and, well, act. The set is for somebody else to do, but I still pay attention so I know what works.

Whether or not I'm a producer on the play, I'm such a stickler for detail. When I am in a new theater, I make a point to go out into different parts of the audience to sit and see what they see. I need to know that everyone can see my movement, and how to hold my face so my reactions can be seen. Because there's no Bill the camera guy swooping in to get that shot. It has to be right there for the person who put down money to watch me act.

The tweaking doesn't stop. Last night we went long, which I had a feeling would happen. So we'll fix that. When you're actually onstage and it's real, you also start to clock stuff in the middle of things. Last night on my way out of a scene, I saw that somebody forgot to take the little price tag off the lamp. So you know I'm gonna go and get that today!

I travel with stage plays, so it's kind of like an old-fashioned theater troupe hitting town. That's different from when you do location work for a film. Then it's like sleepaway camp. There's tons more people and the stars are all kind of forced to hang out together. When I starred as Lysterine in the critically acclaimed *Booty Call*, I worked with the incredible Jamie Foxx. Back then, I knew he was so funny, but oh man, it was hard to be his dressing room neighbor for a few weeks. He had a piano in there, and he would just play it all the time, singing his pretty heart out! One time I was trying to take a nap between scenes, and I went out and screamed at him to stop playing the damn piano, not knowing that in less than ten years he would be getting an Oscar for doing that and so much more in *Ray*.

Getting to work with such talented people is amazing, but travel is also a major aspect to this being my dream job. I feel so blessed to go to these places that Angie from Indianapolis didn't even know existed. Doing *Boat Trip* with Cuba Gooding Jr. brought me to Santorini, Cologne, Israel, Egypt . . . It was just amazing. I did an action comedy with Eddie Griffin that you might have missed called *Blast*. It's the reason I got to go to South Africa for the first time. I distinctly remember looking out at Table Mountain in Cape Town and saying out loud to no one, "Oh my God, I love my life."

(Have I picked a film because of the location? Oh, hell yeah.)

So just as Mary listed her pros, I recognize that acting and producing channels all my gifts and loves. I like being on a team and collaborating as we tell stories I care about. I choose projects that reinforce and extend my personal brand. My OCD tendencies inform my work ethic, or my work ethic is informed by my OCD—it's a chicken-or-egg thing. And I get to pick up and leave, play someone else in some of the most magical places in the world.

It's not enough to decide what you love. Start today on making your dream job happen, not tomorrow.

I recently hosted a baby shower for one of my girlfriends in L.A. I love these kind of events, because it's a time for me to catch up with a lot of my friends all at once. There was this lady, and she just kind of kept looking at me. She was a white woman with brown hair and blond highlights, probably about thirty-five. Finally, I went over and introduced myself.

"I'm so happy to meet you," she said, in this sweet Southern accent. "I wonder if I could get some advice from you."

We sat down and talked. Her name was Colleen, and she told me she had recently moved here from Tennessee. She'd been in pharmaceutical sales and one day decided she wasn't happy. "I stopped my job," she said. "I went back to school and I got my MFA. I studied drama and theater."

"Wow," I said. "It is so important that you studied. I always tell people, you have to be able to do drama, comedy, and musicals. You need to be able to fit in all three."

"I know it could be a little bit late for me," Colleen said, "but I want to be in a movie. Even if I was just an extra, I would be so happy. I want to do what you're doing."

I guess she wanted me to say, "Sure, come to the set next week!" I looked her right in the eye. "You've got to start somewhere," I said. "Don't say 'just an extra,' because that is education. That will get you on a set, and you can see what actors really do. The work isn't just what's on-screen."

Because people just get to see the final version. You don't know that we actors stand on our feet for twelve hours a day. We get hustled through wardrobe changes before we lose the light. We have to learn so many lines and hit our marks *and* look good. Be ready to do a flip and a dip and a hair toss. Most people really don't understand what it is we do.

I asked Colleen what she was doing to make things happen. She said she just got here.

"Well, you can't stand by the pool," I told her. "You have to get in." She's standing there, wondering if it will be cold, fantasizing that it will be warm. She had a head shot, but it was only her seeing it. She needed to get it in front of people. I told her the first thing she needed to do was go to a casting agency. This girl needed to get on a set, fast. She was so worried about starting late that she wasn't starting. Once she's on a set, that is free education. She might see all that work that film actresses do and say, "Hmm." And maybe she will be on a set, being tended to by a third assistant director who's checking the extras' costumes and continuity, and say, "Hey, that's kind of cool." That could be the start of being in charge on a set.

If you want it, you get there. I think of Lupita Nyong'o, the Oscar-winning, Tony-winning fabulous actress. She jumped in that pool when she was visiting family in Nairobi for summer vacation in 2004. She saw a film crew in town and found out they were filming *The Constant Gardener*. "I said, 'I will work for free,'" she recalled saying. "I just had to be on the set." She expressed her ability to help with language barriers. Boom: Hired as a production assistant. On the set. And then she could watch Ralph Fiennes do his thing and ask him questions about his work. One day he asked her what she wanted to do with her life, and she timidly told him she was interested in becoming an actor. "He sighed and said, 'If there's something else that you want to do, do that. Only act if you feel you can't live without it.' It wasn't what I wanted to hear, but it was the thing I needed to hear." That quote is from a 2014 *New York* magazine article called "Lupita Nyong'o, From Unknown to 'It' Girl in Less Than a Year." Less than a year? Not really. She started that ascent nearly ten years before, when she got herself on that first set. And, it must be said, *The Constant Gardener* was not her last production assistant job. You have to put in the work.

I so appreciate that Colleen put time into studying, but I always tell people to educate themselves with real experience. I meet people all the time who say, "I'm going to be the next Viola Davis," or even, "I'm going to be the next Vivica Fox." Not knowing that it took twenty years of work to be Vivica Fox. Or that the amazingly talented Viola Davis got herself to Juilliard and she still wasn't handed a career. She has a two-second scene in her first movie, *The Substance of Fire*, playing a character called "Nurse." She hands someone a vial, but it got her a SAG card. You might think they handed her *Doubt*, knowing she would be brilliant. No. Everyone wanted that role. After auditioning in L.A, she and six other black actresses were brought to a New York soundstage for one day to do a screen test. Each had to go through full hair, makeup, and wardrobe to do a final audition on camera with the crew, director, and producers. She won that role because of her determination and all the small roles she learned from along the way. Her career of excellence didn't happen overnight. *You* know from this book that it didn't happen overnight for me. **Little jobs can lead to big jobs.** I had to get through being green at my first auditions and nervous on my first set, and so does anyone who wants to make it.

Or I'll be on location somewhere in a place that might as well be Timbuktu and a girl will tell me, "I want to be an actress." Then what are you doing in Timbuktu? You have to go where the jobs are if you want to be a working actress. And if you just want to act, then find a regional theater and start doing. I commended Colleen for getting herself to where the action is. Now she just had to be flexible in order to get in the door.

This is true of all professions, not just acting. I have a friend named Doneya who proves it. I met him a few years back when he was the wardrobe assistant on a movie I did for Hallmark. He had a calmness to him, and there's an intimacy to working so closely with an actress, whether it's in wardrobe or makeup. I believe energy is transferable, and if I am about to do a scene, I need someone who isn't bringing bad energy to the job.

Doneya went home to Arizona, and I gave him my email and told him to stay in touch. We talked here and there, and when he was in L.A., we would meet up for lunch sometimes. He was open that he was still figuring out his life and he wondered if he really liked Arizona anymore. "I'm thinking about moving to London or New York."

"Okay, hit me when you get there," I said. Because I wasn't going to finance it. People always want to tell me their dreams and get around to asking me to finance it. Not Doneya.

"I moved to New York!" he wrote a few weeks later. He was staying with a friend and still looking for work as a wardrobe stylist for productions. I told him to keep me posted and let me know he was okay.

Usually when I go to New York, I am in and out for work, but when I realized I was going to be in New York for a few days, I told Doneya I wanted to see him. He wrote back in all caps: "I GOT A NEW JOB!" It was at the Madame Tussauds wax museum. "I love it so much," he said. "Can you please come by?"

Of course I could. We met up for lunch before he gave me a tour, and it was the happiest I've ever seen him. He told me what he'd been through in New York.

"Vivica, I was putting in my résumés everywhere," he told me, "and hearing nothing. I was living off a dollar a day. I would get apples and make a jar of peanut butter and a loaf of bread last forever."

If there was a soup kitchen he could go to, he would. Doneya walked everywhere, never wasting any money on subways, let alone cabs.

"I was down to my last eight cents," he said. He pulled out his phone and showed me a picture he had taken of his bank balance.

"I don't need proof, Doneya," I said. "I believe you, honey."

"No, Vivica, that photo is for me," he said. "I need to look at that so I remember. The night I took that, I said to myself, 'I don't know where tomorrow's gonna lead me.'"

Tomorrow didn't have the answer. Nobody called and gave him a job that day. It doesn't work that way. What he did do was apply to Madame Tussauds, asking if they needed someone to help with wardrobe. He was so excited when they asked him to come in.

When he got there, they said they actually wanted a new makeup artist for the figures. Record scratch, but he was honest. "I don't know how to do makeup," he said. "I do wardrobe, but if you train me, I'll do it."

They liked him—to meet Doneya is to like him—but they just said they would keep him in mind if they needed a wardrobe person.

"Two days later, they called and said their makeup artist quit," he said. "Would I come in and be trained to do the makeup?"

"Hell yeah," I said, grabbing his hand across the table to give it a squeeze.

"Hell yeah," he said. "I got so good at that that I got to do the makeup, hair, and wardrobe."

"Triple threat," I said. "Now you're talking!"

They are so impressed with his work that they are going to fly him to London, and they asked him to assist with the opening of their new museum in Nashville.

"I now have my own place," he said. "I've got benefits. And this is the next chapter."

It's perfect, and it wasn't the obvious choice. **He expanded his reach beyond what he was comfortable with.** He moved past the uncertainty of photo shoots and film sets. He has steady work with all these wax celebrities. He gets to style them and change their looks every once in a while. "It's so creative for me," he told me, and sometimes he gets to meet the actual celebrities. "They'll come in for the openings and I can say, 'Hey, I styled you. I did your makeup and your hair.'"

And nobody's going to come in and say, "Oh, the show got canceled, clear out and good luck."

When the check came, Doneya grabbed it.

"Sweetheart, you don't have to do that," I said.

"Nope," he said. "You've treated me to a lot of lunches. I feel good that I can treat you today."

Here is someone who was down to his last eight cents and he never asked me for a dime. Now he's treating me to lunch! I have a phrase

I use: "Make it do what it do." It's when you make the most of every opportunity and do your best. I say it when I set out to do something, and I say it when I have done just that. "Make it do what it do, Doneya," I said as we left the café. "You did that ish, boy."

Doneya took me on a tour of the museum and showed me his favorites, like Jennifer Lopez and the Ghostbusters Experience. Midway through the tour, I whispered to him. "We need to talk about the hair," I said. "The wigs could be better quality. Do you think on a few of them we could maybe get the Vivica Fox Hair Collection in here? I can't have my girls looking this way."

"What a great idea," he said. "I'll run it by my boss."

"Tell him we'll give you guys a good deal," I said. "And by the way, we need to get a Vivica Fox statue up in here."

I like these stories because they are a contrast in two personality types I see in the hustle, and both have merit. Colleen wanted to do the work of preparation, but was a little iffy on the doing. **What's an action plan without action?** So my advice to her was to just start doing.

Doneya didn't have much prep, but knew that if he could just get in the room, then he'd learn. He stayed flexible, and he found a dream job he didn't know he wanted.

YOU ARE THE BRAND

Now that you have your goal in mind, we need to cover some ground rules for creating and maintaining success. Young people who are just getting out of college often ask me for advice on starting their careers. I always tell them the same thing: Figure out how much debt you're in and come up with some kind of financial plan to get yourself out of debt as quickly as possible. Make sure that the sacrifices you made going to college pay off. Don't get caught up in spending all your money on bling, shoes, and purses. Get a pension plan and a secured, money-generating interest account that is insured. As a member of SAG, I contribute to mine.

That's the basics. Then there is the advanced work of branding yourself. People think a brand is a logo, but it is so much more than that. **Your brand is a promise.** In order to become the go-to first choice for a client or employer, you need to fulfill whatever promise you're making. For me, that promise has been quality.

I have been very successful with branding, and I've learned several lessons along the way. Whether you are an entrepreneur starting a business, or selling the brand of *you* in a business setting, there are definitely rules.

Rule 1: Do your homework.

I hope you're excited and in a rush to get going, but there's some work to do at the outset that you cannot skimp on. Call it the preparty before the main event.

Make sure there's a demand for your brand.

You can't sell ice to Eskimos. They're good, thanks. If you want to open a cupcake shop, don't open it across the street from a beloved bakery. Some call this market research, I call it common sense. Gather a bunch of people you see as your target market, either together in a group or on a bcc email, and ask them questions. Try to get people you don't know into the group, so the answers won't be as predictable or "nice." Ask what they are looking for in a product and what they think a fair price would be. Would they pay three dollars for a cupcake? Do I hear four dollars if they knew it only used organic ingredients? Gather research about their experiences in the bakeries they go to. What would make them come in more often? If you're trying to break into a field but job openings are scarce, ask for an informational interview. What would make a candidate stand out to them? Then you'll know how to pitch yourself.

In my acting and producing career, I have consistently found that mainstream studios undervalue African American theatergoers. That's changing a bit, but through the years I have produced quality projects that didn't just meet that need but created a base of people who know I am looking out for them. I met the demand, and then delivering quality expanded that demand. Now we have to expand the ability of people to see these films by not just opening them in 1,100 theaters but giving them the "typical" wide release of 2,500 theaters. Because not everyone wants to drive forever to see a movie. It prevents these films from reaching certain box office levels, *and* it leaves money on the table.

Look at what your competitors do right—and what they're missing.

If you're starting a business, become an expert in the competition. Sign up for their mailing lists. Study their websites, pricing, and marketing.

Sticking with the cupcake shop idea, go to all the shops in town and test out the experience. What works? Is there no red velvet? Is there no room for girlfriends to sit and eat a cupcake during a four o'clock work break? What's the coffee situation as far as bringing in morning traffic? Find the customers they are neglecting or underappreciating and bring them in.

As I worked on the brand of the Vivica Fox Hair Collection, I saw that there was a general lack of diversity in how wigs and weaves were being marketed. Women of color, especially young women, were not being courted by sellers. It was astonishing, given the huge percentage of African American women who buy these products. I saw an opportunity in representing diversity and inviting the sisters to purchase my products.

Become an "expert."

If I was not an actress and was just starting out with my hair line, I would for damn sure let every reporter in town know I am a resource for them as an expert in hair and beauty trends. Pitch your niche. It's not bragging, it's establishing your credibility as a brand. There is an insatiable need for content these days, and thus an equal need for quotes. Reach out to journalists who cover the work you do or the trends you think your brand can fit into. That article is free advertising, and will lead to the next one and the next one.

Find your money.

When you're approaching potential investors or employers, you need to distill all that homework you're doing down to a brief, confident pitch. This is what they need to know right away: what's the brand and who's the customer. Talk about the money your competitor is leaving on the table by not doing what you can deliver. If it's a job you're after, tell them how investing in you—because a paycheck is an investment—will deliver a return.

Better yet, know that you gotta spend money to make money. If you have saved up some money and you can invest in your brand, guess what, you're gonna reap all the benefits. But if you need to look elsewhere, there are more options than waiting on a Daddy Warbucks to cut you a check. The U.S. government's Small Business Administration is worth checking out. Take their BusinessUSA questionnaire, which will ask you just a few questions about where you live, the nature of the business, and if you fall into any communities eligible for special assistance like veterans and, yes, women. Just like that, it lists state and federal finance programs you might qualify for. Do it!

If you have people who work with you and for you,
make sure that you can trust them.

This isn't just about them running off with your money, though that's important, too. You have to trust that these people take your brand seriously because they are an extension of the brand. If they're the face the customers see when they buy cupcakes on the one day you finally have off, are they a suitable stand-in? Check out their social media, too. You don't want your brand's name in their Instagram bio if they look like they're selling something on the side, okay?

Think like a customer.

As you build the brand of you, step back and put yourself in the shoes of a client or employer. I love putting on my baseball cap and going into one of the beauty shops that sell my products. First off, it's a thrill to see my face on a product, no lie. But these stealth missions show me what it's like for my consumers. How is the presentation? Is the experience fun? How does my product look next to that of another line?

Periodically go on your website and ask yourself if it is looking dated and needs freshening. Make sure it looks good on a mobile device, since that's how so many people will be looking you up. At work, think about how your desk is looking. Make sure the boss sees you working and putting in the hours.

Keep doing market research.

As your website is up and running, check the analytics to see how people are finding you. Are they Googling "best cupcake" or coming in from Twitter? Talk to people about their experiences with you and your brand. Was it positive? If not, what could you have done to fix it? That, by the way, is also a way to save a referral. If you listen and acknowledge a misstep, they may at least recommend you with reservation rather than simply saying, "Steer clear."

No matter what your position is at a company, stay up on how they're doing and how your industry is changing. Don't fall into denial if you see a move toward outsourcing or freelancing out jobs to save money on insurance.

Rule 2: Network like you're already the Head Chick in Charge.

To get some attention and become a player in your field, you're going to need to get out and meet people. Relationships matter, whether they are with your investors, your competition, your clients, or your potential employers.

Right away, start looking for clubs to join. "But Vivica," you might say, "my idea is to make pretty bath soaps. Who the hell has a soap club?" Think bigger, baby. There are meet-ups that cater to female entrepreneurs, small-business owners, and independent artisans.

When you go to these networking events—whether they are breakfasts or cocktail parties—you have to be smart. This isn't just about handing out the business cards you spent so much time on. (I know so many people who think they started a business because they got business cards—don't be one of those nonstarters.) Here are a few guidelines to making the most of those events:

Greet the damn host.

Look, someone wrangled all these cats and dogs into one room, so be sure to thank them for the effort. These people are connectors, and their work continues way after the event they planned. Folks call them all the time: "Do you have an accountant you like?" "I'm looking for a caterer . . ." These connectors pride themselves on their contacts, and even if they have never been a client of yours, they will want to show they can provide an answer and know people in the game.

Do not avoid your competition.

This is not high school and you are not on opposing teams. If you are new on the scene, get to know these people and befriend them. They may need a little sugar, mind you, because nobody likes a newbie marching in, but people want to share what they know. Ask them questions. Maybe there are jobs that they are too busy or not hungry enough to do. Let them know they can send those clients your way. When they do, thank them. I always say the best way to get more is to say thank you.

When I was coming up, I auditioned with the same black actresses over and over. Of course we were in competition. We were six girls in a room going after the same damn role. But if I was standoffish to them, they never would have vouched for me on other projects. When your name comes up, you don't want people shaking their heads.

Embrace your shyness.

I'm not a shy person, but I have some people in my life who are. When I coach them to do something that scares them, I borrow a line from the wonderful Nelson Mandela: "I learned that courage was not the absence of fear, but the triumph over it. The brave man is not he who does not feel afraid, but he who conquers that fear."

So if you're afraid of these events or go and glom onto one person all night, have a plan to move past that. Limit the expectation that you have to meet everyone. You can stay for an hour and meet five people. You can have an icebreaker that states what you obviously fear: "I get so nervous at these things." Do it enough times, and you won't be. And pro tip: Do not drink your nerves away. If you need a prop or something to do with your hands, stick to seltzer! Please, child!

Put on your listening ears.

I can tell when an actor or actress is just waiting for me to finish saying the line so they can say theirs. It's the worst type of acting because there is no natural give-and-take. The same is true at networking events. I know you have your elevator speech planned and you want to talk about your work, but so does the other person. They have a lot to tell you about their success and their mistakes. Learn from them.

Follow up like it's your job.

You know when you think a date went great but you can't be sure until you get The Text? The one that says, "I had a nice time, let's do it again"? Well, you need to send those emails or even old-fashioned note cards that say, "I enjoyed meeting you. Thank you for taking time to talk." Mention what they do so they know it's not a form letter, and say you will keep them in mind if you see any opportunities for them.

Because those business cards you worked so hard on? Chances are they got thrown away. If you hit them with an email, that at least gives you a chance to stay in their contacts if someone ever asks for a referral.

Don't overpay to play.

When you get a little bit of success, you start getting invited to these big dinners and awards nights that on paper look like a great place to network. These invites can cost three hundred dollars and up! After you go to a few, you realize that you really just get the cocktail hour to network, and then it's hard to see anyone once you're seated for the presentation. Is it worth the investment? It might be better to pinpoint a specific person—even the person getting the award—and invite them to lunch. Then you'll have their undivided attention, and they'll understand you value their time enough to buy them a meal. Three hundred dollars is a *lot* of lunches.

Rule 3: Put social media to werq.

I posted my very first Instagram in June 2012, just a few months after Kim Kardashian. I say that not because I was copying Kim but to give you context on how early I started since you know that girl knows social media. It had taken me a minute to see what a tool Twitter could be for my branding and for my advocacy, and I wasn't going to make that mistake again.

A few months after I joined, I was hanging with a celebrity and she saw me take a selfie.

"Isn't that like another job?" she said. "We have to look good all the time?"

"No," I said, checking my angles and liking what I saw. "That's what Valencia is for." I was joking about the filter—one that I love, by the way—but I see social media as a great way to connect with fans and tell them about my projects. As far as excellent advertising and brand management, Instagram completely took my hair collection to another level. It provided a way to not just show people the styles, but also turn them into customers by telling them where to go to get the looks for themselves.

The question is no longer "Should I do social media?" because the answer is yes. Here are some better questions to ask yourself:

Where is your audience?

Is your client base more likely to be on Twitter, Facebook, or Instagram? My work is very visual—fashion, beauty, and entertainment—so Instagram is great for me. But it is easier for me to share notes and respond to people on Twitter. If a girl in Topeka tweets that she is about to watch a movie I'm in, I want to say thank you. It makes her feel special, and it shows all my fans, "Hey, I see you, and I love you." So I devote energy to both.

What's trending?

I confess I get a little competitive about what's scoring high on the Twitter board. One night *Empire* was trending number two behind something to do with the last election and I was like, "Come on! Take it!" Use hashtags to join big conversations so you can get a lot of eyes on your posts.

What can you offer?

It can't be about business all the time. If my feeds were all "New show" and "New wig!" all the time, people would just tune me out and say, "Sell it someplace else, sister." Show your authentic self as you make that honest connection. Just don't overshare. Don't be lying in bed or showing too much skin. Because then what are you advertising? People also need to realize that once you put something out on social media, it's there forever. You can't take it back.

Be sure also to promote other people's projects so they will repost. It's an opportunity for you to connect with their followers and turn them into your customers, too.

Are you going to be consistent?

Nothing dustier than a tweet from last year and sadder than an Instagram feed of three pics. The more you post, the more followers you get, so make a point to open big and post consistently.

Who do you—and your brand—emulate?

I love inspirational quotes and I know I am not alone. If you're looking to define your brand, give people clues to who you are by quoting people who have already established their brand in that field. What does it say about me as a businesswoman if I quote Lee Iacocca, a legend in the automobile business? "Get all the education you can, but then, by God, do something," he once said. "Don't just stand there, make it happen." Yaaaass! I cosign that by posting it, and in a way Iacocca cosigns my brand. I will give you a Vivica Fox quote I always love to lay on people: "Versatility has been the key to my longevity." Put *that* on a pretty picture of me and send it out to the world, honey.

Rule 4: Lead by example.

As you build success, you are going to have employees or staff to manage. The boss sets the tone for the organization and for the day. If you're slow to make decisions or you waffle, that's going to be how everyone operates. If you speak to people in a nasty manner or share too much about your personal life, then you are giving your employees permission to do the same.

Because I am so punctual, that trickles down so that the people who work with me know they have to be punctual, too. Or else they won't be working with me. If I am going to be late, I am the person who will let you know where I am at—"Hey, can I get another fifteen minutes?"—because I respect other people's time. Nothing pisses me off more than somebody who is constantly late.

I take that back. I hate laziness more. I have a tremendous work ethic and I try to inspire that in the people I hire. I had a makeup artist who I gave an opportunity of a lifetime to work on a show with me. We went on hiatus, but I had several photo shoots lined up to promote the show. Mind you, she was getting paid for this work, but I wasn't because I was doing it for the show.

As I was telling her the schedule, she made a face. "Are we *ever* going to get any time off?" she said.

I looked at her for a second. "Sure," I said. "When your check stops coming, you're going to sho' nuff get some time off. Sound good?"

When you want to expand your brand beyond just one job, you have to change your definition of "time off." I look at people like Beyoncé and Jennifer Lopez—when you're in the music industry and trying to make movies, you work all the time. I find that around Christmastime, no one works. I rest then.

I'm not saying you can't have a life, but you got to strike while the iron's hot.

Rule 5: Know your brand's worth.

You're going to have to get past any squeamishness about negotiating deals or asking for raises. Just do it intelligently. First of all, I know my worth, but I'm not a bitch. It's an unfortunate reality that men can go about asking for things differently, but it's getting better. However, a woman can and should put her foot down, and say, "Hey, we're entitled to equal pay." We're only finding it out now in Hollywood. "Oh, shit? For years we weren't getting paid the same as guys? And we were doing the same amount of work?" They keep it secret on purpose, and since we get so hung up talking about money, it stays hidden. I think it's so important that we talk about this and expose it so that we can have equality. Jennifer Lawrence wrote a powerful essay about it for Lena Dunham's *Lenny* newsletter after she found out "lucky people with dicks" like Bradley Cooper got a bigger payday for costarring in *Silver Linings Playbook*. "I didn't get mad at Sony," she wrote. "I got mad at myself. I failed as a negotiator because I gave up too early."

It was my manager, Lita, who clued me in on reading the fine print. I remember we were doing a deal I was so excited about, and I just wanted to get the negotiation part over with so I could show I was a team player.

"Okay, we've got to start paying attention," Lita told me.

"Let's sign the contract and let's go."

"Just so you know, it's probably going to take me a few days to read it."

"What?" I said. "Just look at the dollars and the cents and then sign it."

"No, Vivica," she said. "Nope, nope, nope. I want you to know everything you are signed up for and what you are entitled to."

I appreciate her doing that. Don't be afraid to know your worth and what you should be paid. And there are some jobs you know as an actress that if it's an independent project, the paycheck is going to be different. If it is a project that you know is going to be special, then make that choice. But if it's a franchise, then you need to benefit from the full rewards of what your work has done. You have to show you are aware that the reason they are making a sequel is *you*.

Never be afraid to ask for a raise, but be smart about how you do it. If the company is successful and everyone is doing good and smiling, go for it. You know when your company ain't doing well, trust me. If you see other people kind of getting promotions and you're doing all the hard work, you've got to sit down and have a discussion and not be afraid to say, "I'm doing a lot of work . . ." just to make sure you're not being taken advantage of. And if you feel like you are, make a plan B and keep it moving.

Rule 6: Learn from "No."

You have the opportunity to learn from every experience, even negative ones. When you are told no—whether it's not getting a job or not winning over a client—examine the lesson. When I don't get a role I thought I was right for, I ask myself why. Was I ready? Did I prepare myself? Did I show up with a good attitude? Then I look at the person who did get the job. Sometimes it's the type. I might have been too damn tall. They might have wanted someone who had a different look than I have. And that's okay. Because everything is not for you. And I find that if you have more grace, you learn. *That gig wasn't for me.*

Feel free to ask for pointers from the people who gave you that no. Assure them that you're not asking anybody to change his or her mind, but merely want to see what you could do differently in the future. You will at least profit from the knowledge.

REMEMBER HOW TO HAVE A GOOD TIME

know, I know, "TGIF" stands for "The Grind Includes Friday." But I want you to keep your sanity, too. Your soul needs replenishing while you're doing all this work. So remember that your squad is not just for networking. I am blessed to have a close circle of friends who cheer me on and cheer me up. You also need to avoid becoming so laser-focused on your goals that you ignore your friends.

If I am not on location or traveling, Sunday is usually my day of rest and recharge. (And it just happens to be my cheat day when I am dieting!) Years back, I became famous in my circle for hosting my Football Sundays. I started inviting people to come over for tacos and mimosas, and to watch football.

Football Sundays had a family feel, like an old-fashioned block party back in Indy. Sit wherever, and if you need anything, help yourself. I'd always have a game on, and I gave shy people jobs so they'd warm up and have something to talk to people about. The only requirement for an invite was that I liked you, so the crowd was naturally diverse, with friends from all parts of my life. Some were Hollywood folk, some owned their own businesses, and some were just cool people. And yes, it was an opportunity for people to make business connections with people they wouldn't usually be sharing a meal with. I know there were some love connections made at my Taco Sundays, too.

This routine gathering worked so well for me because I could spend quality time with a lot of people at once. When you're busy, you hear a lot of "We need to catch up" and "We need to do lunch." You could drown in those needs because you and I know that you eat through lunch and work until midnight. Setting a reliable time in your calendar to get your circle together is a great way to check in on them and make sure you have a set time to recharge with fellowship.

People sometimes want to host gatherings but think they have to impress people with elaborate and extravagant meals. They work themselves to the bone, waste a lot of money, and don't have a good time. Their guests don't either. They stand there awkwardly, worriedly offering to help, and then can't have a real conversation until they are in the car saying, "Never again!" **It's better to have a simple gathering and understand that you and the good people you invite are the draw.** The food and the price tag are completely secondary to the luxury of friendship.

You don't need a big place either. I know a young woman in New York who has a group of about five or six friends who meet every two months for something they call Champagne & Chipotle. Whoever's turn it is to host orders the burritos, and each guest just has to bring an inexpensive bottle of prosecco—or a nice bottle of champagne if they're doing well! What's great is that they all started at the same ad agency, and each has gone on to other places, and one has even started her own agency. They can compare notes and experiences with people who have their backs.

Another cool way for people to gather to talk when you're mind-ing a budget is choosing a restaurant where everyone pays their own way. Upscale cafeteria-style restaurants are becoming increasingly popular, and they help you avoid the six separate checks or, worse, the dreaded math of "Well, you had a cappuccino . . ." Because not everyone has a Vivica to pick up the check for the group. Remem-ber, your Vivica doesn't want to always be picking up the check either.

I eventually hung up my hosting sombrero and started doing more laid-back Sundays with a few of my girls. I can plan the ultimate girls' night if I need to, but I prefer to have girls' days. If we're really doing it up, we start the day at a spa, but no matter what we always do brunch. I like a restaurant near my house. It has beautiful views and plenty of televisions so we can watch the game. I could watch foot-ball all day. Seriously, you can have breakfast food, take a breather, have some lunch food, and then watch sports. I tell my girls, "Let's get together and just hang. Have a bottle of Chardonnay and watch these boys in these tight white pants run around and be athletic."

I order huevos rancheros with a side of bacon if I'm not being too careful. And definitely fresh-squeezed orange juice. Don't give me no concentrated, because once you have fresh-squeezed orange juice, there's no going back. The only way I'll drink concentrated is if I can kill it with champagne!

Birthdays are very important to me, and for the past few years I have celebrated the occasion with a trip to Montego Bay on the north coast of Jamaica. It's the only place I can go to relax. I just have a special thing with the blue of the water there. I want a beach where I can watch the sunset, have a drink, and be thankful.

I like to bring my family and best friends, because it's part of shar-ing my success. I love that the Lord has afforded me the luxury that I can take my friends and family. They say, "Girl, how much?" And

I am like, "I got you." I work hard so I can play even harder and have some of my loved ones share in the fun.

I love to see my sister, Sug, bloom in Jamaica. It's a small way to pay her back for all the responsibility she had to have taking care of us Fox kids when she was little. She was reluctant at first because she is light-skinned and growing up she didn't really like the sun so much. She skipped the first trip, but once she saw how much fun we were having, she called me.

"I am not being left ashore next year!" she said. Sure enough, she was in for the following year. "I'm gonna have me a good time."

Oh, and she does. I remember once looking around saying, "Where'd Sugie go?"

"Hieeee," I heard. She was at the hotel bar, just loving life. "This is the best!" she yelled.

"No, you are!" I said.

As you grow more successful, you'll want to share that joy with the people who have given you joy. I see some girls make it and there's a diva selfishness that poisons them and their relationships: "I'm here and I'm not sharing this space with anybody." It always bothers me when I see girls who have that kind of energy. You want to tell them, "Sister, just so you know, they're gonna use you for so long, and then they're gonna use you up. If you have ostracized yourself from everybody—people gonna remember that."

They say it's lonely at the top? Well, honey, it can be even lonelier when your time is over and you haven't shared any of your blessings. Then who will share their blessings with you?

TURN YOUR HATERS INTO CONGRATULATORS

We live in a comment culture now. Social media means that everyone can say anything they want and there's no time to worry about feelings.

If something is off, they will let your ass know immejiately on Instagram. Not immediately. *Immejiately.* When something ain't working, they comment: "No no no no no. Hell no. What were you thinking? No, ma'am."

I like that they are candid and straight with me, but sometimes I want to say, "Ain't your mama ever taught ya that if you ain't got nothing nice to say, don't say nothing at all?" Not these kids. Nope. And then you go to their pages and, surprise, they're private.

The other night I thought I slayed them at a premiere in my black leather Versace dress and Versace heels. I have been taking risks with color, so I went with this long fuchsia hair that I loved. I got a great response at the party, but when I posted a picture, some girl commented: "You just fucked yourself up trying to look young."

I can usually take it, but I wondered what about my outfit, which was in no way scandalous, said that I was trying to look too young? I'll own it—I looked good. Then I realized that they just don't think a fifty-something woman should be allowed to feel beautiful. Or maybe even exist. They used to put all us actresses out to pasture, but here we are. And I also thought, *You're just jealous because you can't afford this dress.* I blocked the girl, and I couldn't pick her out of a lineup to save my life.

As you become the person you are meant to be, people will want to drag you down because they are jealous. Whether it's the success in your career or your love life, they will covet what you have. **If they can't take success and its trappings from you, they want to steal the joy that success gives you.** Take it as a compliment. A hater is actually a congratulator, pointing out your riches. "Who does she think she is?" is the only way their minds can reconcile this fear: "She *must* think she's better than me, because *I* think she is better than me."

This chapter is about troubleshooting the relationships in life and business that success can sometimes complicate.

1. Take off your Captain Save-a-Ho cape.

Understand that a lot of people will have a hand out once you make it. As I started reaping the rewards of my hard work, there were some people who felt they were entitled to a share in the profits. I have to warn you, once people know you can pay your own bills, some want you to pay theirs. I cannot stress this enough: Don't do it.

It took me a long time to learn that I had to take off my Captain Save-a-Ho superhero cape. I used to say, "Oh, you need a new car?" "Oh, you need ten thousand dollars?" And I would never see any of it come back. They would be like, "Oh, she's making money. She doesn't need it."

Three years ago I took off my Captain Save-a-Ho cape. I had to, because everybody was sucking and dragging my nipples down to the damn ground. I was providing for others and not getting anything back. I wasn't even getting back gratitude. But I still slip. I helped a friend of mine get a car. I was her cosigner, and I ended up having to make four or five payments for her. The other day, this lady creditor called me, super polite. "Miss Fox, she only owes seven hundred more dollars," she said. "She's sixty days' delinquent."

She told me that because it was out of state I could only pay cash. So I went to the bank and got the money. Do you know who has called me to say thank you? The freaking creditor. "I just want you to know the loan is paid in full, Miss Fox," she said. "No more problems. You won't be hearing from us again. Thank you for making sure that whenever we needed to let you know that the loan was falling behind that you always responded and you helped us out. I wish you the best." Did my friend wish me the best? NO!

Another friend, this one from high school, called me and said that she wanted her daughter to try something from my hair line and asked if I could also send a dress. I tell you, now that I've got a clothing line and a hair line, people think I'm just sitting around in a house full of wigs and gowns. Vivica Claus with boxes and boxes in my garage! Um, no. But I didn't tell her that. I went to a store to buy the hair for the weave and picked out an outfit—you know I like to see what the customer experiences when they buy my products. The hair alone was $138, and on top of that the FedEx bill was $40.

A week went by. Do you know I had to text her to ask if she got the package? "Oh yeah," she said. "I have been meaning to thank you."

Bitch, all you had to do was text.

And so I resolved to stop having nonreciprocal relationships. I am a good friend, and I want my loved ones to be able to ask me for help when they fall on hard times. But if you find yourself being around people where *all the time* it's hard for them? And they ain't doin' nothin' for you? You might want to think twice about that relationship. What are you in it for? Give them a time-out. It's not just about money. You can make more money. It's about your time, your care, your love.

When you get older, you learn that what Maya Angelou said was exactly right: When people show you who they are, believe them. I'm in my damn fifties and I only recently learned this about friendship. I owe this lesson to my wonderful assistant Darren. One day I was at my house with him, fuming about someone being ungrateful about a loan I knew would never be returned. I went on and on and then he suddenly stopped me.

"Vivica," he said, "you don't have to pay people to be your friend."

"I don't do that," I said.

"Yes, you do," he said. "You think you're giving them what they need, but you're just giving them what they want. All they should really need is your friendship."

It sounds so simple, but it was a real revelation. I remember resting my chin on my palm and really giving it a think.

"And is it friendship if you do for them," he asked, "and then you get mad and run around cussin'? Just don't do for them then."

My palm went from my chin to cover my eyes. How many times had my true friends sat through these tales of ungrateful people? I could have been talking about the great person in front of me, not the ungrateful person who had disappointed me. Not only was I out that money, I let them steal joy from my time with other people.

I believe in you. You're reading this book because you want to invest in your future. I have to caution you that when you become a success, you will be a target for lazy people. They see that someone just handed you a million dollars. They don't realize that there are taxes, agents, overhead . . . I see some people in my profession develop expensive habits right away. Like diamonds and cars and parties and groupies and hangers-on. And the next thing you know, you're broke. And where's your next million dollars?

And get ready, because everybody comes to you with "great plans." I had some guy hint at that just the other day in an email: "You know, I'm really trying to get my clothing line business off the ground, but I just don't have the resources . . ." I wish him the best, but I didn't even respond to him. I read it and said to myself, *Dude, I guess you're gonna figure it out like I did.*

It is so much better to invest in a real charity. For me, giving back is therapeutic. You have to have some time when it's not about you or your career. I have been involved with Best Buddies for over fifteen years, after being introduced to their work by my friend Carl Lewis, the Olympic champion track runner. Best Buddies helps people with intellectual and developmental disabilities find job opportunities, housing, and one-to-one mentors. It's my kind of organization because it creates self-advocates and puts people to work. When you see these amazing, beautiful people become so happy over being able to have an apartment, work, and engage in the world, it makes you want to invest in them. I don't have special needs, but I know how hard the struggle was when I left home at seventeen to start my career. These worker bees have the same happiness I have about being able to wake up in my home and go out to do work that matters to me.

I am so proud that I was able to raise $70,000 for them while I was on *Celebrity Apprentice*. I remember while I was doing the show I took some kids from the program to lunch. Seeing their smiling faces, I thought, *I am going to make you some money.* By the way, if this book helps put you in a position to hire people, please, *please* look into Best Buddies' jobs program. The organization will give you the support you need as you present someone with an opportunity for work and independence. Trust, you and your business will be rewarded as you witness this person's passion, ability, and motivation.

Put your hard-earned money in an organization like that, not some lazy cousin's new car.

2. Stand still and the snakes will reveal themselves.

Not everyone is so happy to see *you* so happy. I have learned a valuable lesson about letting people tell you who they are. If you stand still and take a moment to really look at your relationships with people, the snakes will slither around you and reveal themselves.

Think for a moment about your friendships. Are there some underminers in your midst, actively trying to keep you from succeeding? The saboteurs are not always the obvious ones, but I find they show themselves when we are making positive changes in our lives.

I had one girlfriend who I used to hang out with a lot, and the end of every meet-up was like a weary sigh. One time I was driving back home from a dinner date with her, and I realized she always left me feeling more negative about myself than positive. If I didn't get a job, oh, she wanted to really examine that crime scene. Make me feel like I was robbed, but ask a lot of questions about what I thought I did wrong. Suddenly, a small gig that I wasn't the right fit for was like some huge loss. But if I was excited about a project, really bursting to talk about it, she'd start talking about herself or say something like, "Girl, all this work stuff—I don't know when you're going to find time to meet a guy."

She used passive-aggressive comments to make me feel small. We need to be cheerleaders for each other. When you hang up the phone with your friend or leave a brunch, the spirit has to be "You got this!" The impulse was to cut her out, but instead I took a break from her. It let me examine why I was seeing so much of her. I realized it was comfortable. We had a script, and the dialogue was tired.

I find these negativity folks to be the most common type of underminers. The truly bad ones, who I have zero time for, actively tell you that you won't succeed. Sometimes people in our lives like to beat up our egos because they think it keeps us in our place. I can't have that. If someone goes out of his or her way to make you feel anything less than special—I am talking blessed and highly favored—shut that down. Let's run a drill:

"Don't be thinking you're special."

"No, bitch, I *am* special. And I'm fabulous. And if you don't get it, get away from me."

Because we all need to hear compliments. I'm not saying that we're all needy for assurance. You gotta have some confidence in yourself that when you put yourself forward, you've got faith in yourself and your talent. But especially if you're in the business of performing, if that person—a friend, a colleague, a lover—isn't a source of support and positive reinforcement, you might want to think about that.

You deserve the best. If your best friend is not your rock, your ace boon coon that's got your back like no other? Drop them.

3. Don't let someone ruin your workplace.

Do you have a snake on the loose in your office? My condolences, but we'll get through this. These are the coworkers who are all smiles talking about wanting to hear your ideas—because we're all working together, right? Then they take the good ones and shoot down the ones where they won't be the hero.

I was working with this one gentleman who was in over his head on a production. He acted like the president of the Vivica Fox Fan Club, always saying he wanted my opinion—that is, until I actually gave my opinion. I offered a constructive suggestion on how he could speed something up to avoid overtime on set. He felt threatened, and boy, did the real him come out.

It didn't surprise me, but it was disappointing. I normally would have argued with him and all that. But I sat my ass down and instead of wasting words on him, I spoke to myself.

Let me tell you what you are gettin' ready to do, I said. *This is not gonna stress you out. You gonna sit your butt down, play your position, and stay in your lane. Watch this unfold, and when it starts happening where he's paying overtime, then he'll know what you tried to tell him.*

Sometimes you have to let people fall on their faces if they don't want to take your advice. Don't argue with them about what you know is going to happen. Just sit back and relax and enjoy the show.

There's a phrase my mama uses for letting people find something out the hard way: "They don't think fat meat greasy." Fat meat is greasy the way the sky is blue. And you can deny a fact all you want, but once you bite into that fat meat, you and your hard head are gonna know.

Sometimes holding your tongue is the best offense *and* defense for a jerk at work. I worked with one actor who was just nasty to people on the set. He demeaned newcomers and treated production assistants like personal attendants. And so I simply stopped speaking to him. I didn't say a single word to this actor unless it was in dialogue. He got the message right quick, and he later approached me at a party and apologized.

If you have someone like that at work, try to have as little to do with them as possible. If you have advance warning that this person is trouble, imagine you have garlic and a crucifix, and keep them away from the get-go.

A lot of my girlfriends tell me stories about these "Whoops, did I not cc you?" types in the office. You know why they don't include you. They're cutting you out of decision making to weaken your influence in the office, or they are likely presenting your idea as theirs. With them, you have to drag them into the town square right away so everyone knows what's up. It sends a signal that you know what's going on in your office—don't even try to have a meeting without me, sneak—and everyone will know it's no accident when it happens again. Be up front. As my dad used to tell me, "Don't let someone piss down your back and tell you it's raining."

Make sure you keep a record of everything in case you have to present the receipts! Mind your own receipts, too. There are too many electronic trails nowadays, so make sure you're not talking on some instant messenger, thinking you're cute bitching about a co-worker. Don't email or text anything you wouldn't be comfortable with your boss seeing.

If you have to go to your boss about a coworker, do not make it their problem to solve. Then guess who's the face of the problem? You. Now, you and I know the reason you are going to your boss is to put them on notice that your coworker is a trick bag ho who doesn't like you. But you can't say that. You *can* say, "Hey, I don't want to make this your problem, but this person's actions are affecting the work flow here." Use concrete examples and don't make it personal. For heaven's sake, don't say, "They go or I go." First off, giving a boss an ultimatum is never smart. Second, it's hard work firing someone. If you're offering to politely walk yourself out the door to solve the issue with no confrontation for them, your boss just might take you up on that offer.

As you work out what you're going to say, also think about what will happen *after* you leave your boss's office. The goal should be that your coworker will now be held accountable for their negative actions. If you just vented about someone, your boss might say, "Well, that was a waste of ten minutes." If you got dramatic, your boss is going to wonder how any work is getting done. But if you play it right, stay professional, and keep it about business, the boss will say, "That person managed the situation."

Because in the end, a boss has to care about the company first, and you're maybe somewhere down the list. Make it about helping the business run smoothly, not your life.

4. Sometimes even your family needs the long-handled spoon.

Look, I love my family. I am blessed to have them in my life. But we all know that sometimes when you love someone so deeply, they can hurt you or distract you without meaning to. So now and then you have to treat people with the long-handled spoon. It's an old phrase that means that every once in a while you need to keep your distance a little.

I know a lot of people have small mother-daughter conflicts, and of course I am no different, Everlyena and I are human. She can be my hero and still be human. For a long time, I think she feared that I would become full of myself. She worried that success would make me arrogant or forget to thank the Lord for the blessings He has given me. To keep me humble, she didn't celebrate my achievements in high school. When my team won the city championship, she wasn't even there. My dad cheered double on her behalf.

I resented it for a long time. When my career was really getting super hot, she went through a phase of saying, "Don't be gettin' on that high horse." Well, I kind of earned that high horse. I was proud to be up there, and I wanted to extend my hand to bring her up there with me. And I felt she batted it away.

I would ask her if she saw something of mine on TV, and she would offer a vague "If you don't call and tell me it's on . . ." I just wanted her to say she saw it and I was pretty. Or I would send her clothing from a shopping spree because she won't go shopping herself.

"Mom, did you get the outfits I sent?"

"Yeah, I got 'em, but some of them things . . . Uh, I don't know."

She didn't know then that what I craved so much, all my life really, was simply her approval. A few years back, I learned to stop looking for that from her. If she said she was proud of me, it was because she truly was, not because I badgered it out of her. The long handle of the spoon gave me perspective. Our relationship improved.

The long-handled spoon goes both ways, mind you. Sometimes we have to step back and say, "You know, I am not going to tell you how to live your life." My dad and I were incredibly close. He saw everything I did, and he told me all the time how proud he was to be my father. "That's my baby," he said. "I watched you, you're looking good."

His health was not great as I wrote the book. I visited him because I was concerned that he was becoming isolated with his wife. He wasn't reaching out to us Fox kids. But when I saw how much he depended on her, truly wanted her to be at his side in a time of crisis, I realized I had to respect that. I selfishly wanted to be the one to help him, and if it couldn't be me, then I felt damn sure it should have been a Fox kid. I had to get over it and show how much I loved him by respecting whom he loved.

Step back and examine your family relationships. If expecting them to change isn't working, try changing your expectations.

5. Be woman enough to apologize.

I am the first to admit I am not perfect. I once had to ask the forgiveness of two friends who I had flat-out wronged. It happened when I got caught up in the dreaded best friend contest. It's when your girlfriends fight over who is closer to you. As a celebrity, I am particularly vulnerable to it. But then I did it myself!

At the time my girlfriend Azja was starting this thing with a weight-loss company just as she got a new boyfriend. She was busy with both all the time, and I insecurely felt like I was losing her. I complained about it to my dear friend Jazsmin, who sympathized.

Then one night, maybe after a glass of wine—okay, definitely after a glass of wine—I went on Instagram and saw a picture of them together. Azja wrote, "My new client!" I got into my feelings. I had it in my fool head that Jazsmin was somehow cheating on me by helping with this business.

I wrote a scathing email. A truly ugly letter talking about how I had connected them in the first place and asking them why they were going behind my back. I have to own that regret, and I got what I deserved. They didn't speak to me for a full year. I continually apologized and the response was, "Nope, not accepted."

When I lost that friendship, I made a promise to myself that if I ever found myself feeling a certain kind of way about a friend, I would say, "Hey, let's talk about this. This is how you're making me feel." Because there's two sides to every story. Maybe it wasn't that person's intention to make you feel that way or to hurt your feelings. And maybe that day you were hypersensitive and didn't have the right perspective.

They finally accepted my apology, and I accepted the lesson that came with saying I was wrong. I just didn't understand that new chapter for Azja. Now she's engaged and I love her fiancé. They are going to have a wonderful life together. But I made it about me losing her. I was too in her business. You've got to let your friends grow. Never say, "My way or the highway," because that doesn't make you a good friend.

PART THREE

A TROUBLE-SHOOTING GUIDE TO THE HEART

IF YOU CHASE THAT WEDDING RING, YOU'RE GONNA TRIP

Here's a really bad reason to get married: because everyone else is doing it. I know that's why I did it. It seems like a blink-and-you-missed-it marriage to a lot of people now, but in 1998 I went into a four-year union that I had no business going into. I got married out of peer pressure and because I thought that was the next thing on the checklist of what it means to be a successful woman. I didn't take time to get to know him.

Let me take you back to December 19, 1996. I had just wrapped *Soul Food*, which we shot primarily in Chicago, and I was so happy to be back in warm, beautiful Los Angeles. My girls wanted to go out to celebrate my homecoming, so we headed to Bar One night-club in Beverly Hills.

The girls and me were hanging and catching up on the various story lines of each other's lives when this *six-foot-nine* guy comes up to us.

"Are you Vivica Fox?"

"Yeah," I said.

"Wow," he said, "you're even better-looking in person."

Oh, vanity. I fell for it, but I'm a girl's girl, and I didn't want a guy to get in the way of a ladies' night.

"You're a warm brother," I said, "but I have to go."

I took the girls out onto the dance floor like we had an important meeting or I was Cinderella. As I was dancing, I'd sneak looks—he kind of stood out with that height—and the guy wasn't budging.

My friends wanted to get drinks, so I went back to the bar, purposefully not looking his way. He left and I thought, *Fool, you played yourself playing hard to get.* But he came back. He bought twenty roses from one of those flower guys who hang outside clubs. Some other guys started trying to talk to me, but he hung in, just handing me these twenty roses, one by one. It had been so long since I had been wooed. It worked.

I let him move in to my house four months later. I was truly in love. He proposed one year to the day that we met, December 19. I had been chasing that ring, honey, and I expected it for sure.

The night of the proposal he took me out to dinner and, oh, that meal was the worst. The whole time at the restaurant, there was me expecting him to take a knee at any moment. Every time a waiter brought a glass or a dish, I'd look for a ring. By the time we got in the car, I'd gone through all the stages of grief in my head: denial, anger, bargaining, depression, and acceptance.

Oh well, I thought as I looked in my reflection in the passenger-side window, *maybe I'm expecting too much.*

We got home and I saw the place was filled with roses and candles. He had asked my assistant to decorate the house with roses and scented candles while we went out to dinner. He got down on one knee and presented the ring. I was crying so much that I had to blink my eyes at the ring in the candlelight. I couldn't see straight!

"What color is it?" I yelled, squinting. "You know I don't like gold!"

He laughed, thank God. "It's platinum," he said. "Your favorite."

I checked the box marked "Get an engagement ring" on my list of life goals. Then I got started on the next to-do I thought I was supposed to fulfill: plan a dream wedding that wows everyone.

We had our wedding exactly one year later, keeping our devotion to good old December 19. I had it at the Park Plaza in Los Angeles, an Art Deco palace used as a film set for old-Hollywood-type movies and as a venue by brides who want an over-the-top Cinderella wedding. Guilty as charged.

I really went for it. I even arrived in a horse-drawn carriage decorated with flowers and white organza and sparkling little lights. A paparazzo falling out of a tree delayed my big entrance. Someone freaked and called an ambulance, but he was okay.

We invited 260 people, including Madame King, the woman who put me in my very first fashion show. She was the biggest celebrity in my heart, but we also had Magic Johnson and Shaq, as well as my girls Holly Robinson Peete, Lela Rochon, and Tisha Campbell-Martin. I wore an ivory Escada gown that I kept sleek because I was terrified of looking like a poufy debutante. I wore my hair upswept, and you know I had the veil and crown. I also had my six bridesmaids in Escada, but I gave them Reebok sneakers with silver trim to change into for the reception. I needed no excuses for why they couldn't be on the dance floor with me.

Jeffrey Johnson, one of my boys from Arlington High, had become a pastor, so he married us. My mom loved that. Tisha serenaded us with "The First Time Ever I Saw Your Face," and Tichina Arnold sang the Lord's Prayer a cappella.

During dinner, we had this slideshow of pictures of us separate from age three, moving up until we were a couple. I looked at the face of little Angie, growing up into Vivica, and I was so proud. I caught Madame King's eye, and she said, "Look at you."

At the reception, my husband serenaded me with a song, "The Love You Give," which talks about roses. Then they pulled back a curtain and there were two giant vases of a thousand long-stemmed roses.

I checked the box that said "Perfect wedding."

Then real life began. I was miserable. I hate to say it, but I was just miserable. After the first year, I knew I had made a mistake. But I stayed, and that huge house began to feel like a big ol' prison that I had built for myself.

My husband was very comfortable watching me work and be the breadwinner, and didn't seem to have any idea about "our" finances. Money was just there. Now, do not get it twisted: If you're blessed that your significant other makes real money, that's awesome. But in a true partnership, each has to contribute in some way. Otherwise, you are inviting resentment to just come into your life and make itself comfortable. Resentment will work its way into every little interaction you have with your partner. That's what happened to me.

The first time I tried to talk about it, I had let that resentment back up so it came out fast and furious. It happened when my husband and I were picking out an outfit for him to wear to a premiere we were attending. At the store, he announced that he needed a new pair of black shoes.

"You've got three pairs of black shoes at home," I said.

"But I want some new ones," he said.

I nodded my head, and I remember saying to him, so that no one else could hear us, "I'm getting really sick of me breaking out my credit card all the time."

He paused and shook his head. "Damn," he said. "It hurts me as much as it hurts you."

Even then, I thought, *What the hell? I have to pay for your shoes, your food, and the house, but we can't simply acknowledge that fact because your ego is fragile?*

I heard my mother's voice in my head: "Angie, I didn't raise you to take care of a man."

I knew I would only resent my husband more if I wasn't honest with him. At home I sat him down and told him that I needed help carrying the load. He talked about getting out there to hustle for work and budgeting more. I thought, *Okay, we can go on from here.* But it only lasted a little while, and soon he was back to his habits. It became a cycle, with me asking for help from him, and him trying for a short while. That resentment built up to a point where there was simply no room for love.

When being honest with him didn't create change, I had to be honest with myself. We were living in a house with five bedrooms and eight bathrooms. Our overheard was $12,000 a month. In the last year of our marriage, I was training for *Kill Bill* without getting paid. I had about $200,000 in the bank, and I just watched it whittle down while he didn't seem to notice. He was not concerned at all.

There was an exact moment when I made a decision. It was after driving home after a long day of *Kill Bill* training. I walked into my house, completely sore and drained. The TV was on, and I stood in the doorway. The words I said silently to myself and God were, *Lord, I don't want to do this no more.*

I had fallen out of love with him, and I grieved that. But I don't believe in living miserably. I talked to my assistant Darren, who always knows just what to say.

"I'm not happy," I said. I think I needed someone to tell me it was okay to leave him, and he saw right through that.

"You decide what you're gonna do," he said. "It's going to be on you."

Darren was right, of course. My husband was not about to end this, so it was on me to do it. Soon after, I got a letter from a real estate agent saying that there was a lot of interest in my house. The community around me had built up on a hill, and my home had the most spectacular view. The letter said that if I ever wanted to sell . . .

Darren was there when I got the letter.

"Darren," I screamed, "there is a God and He is good!"

I put the place on the market, and just as soon as I did, Quentin Tarantino dropped the bomb on us that we all had to go to China to continue our martial arts studies. Initially, it was just going to be Uma Thurman going, but now we all had to go. I admit I was really put out about it. So after a horrific number of hours in the air, I landed in China at the crack of dawn, exhausted.

Just as I'd fallen asleep in my hotel room, the phone started going. Lord. It was Darren.

"Darren, you know I have been freaking traveling forever," I said. "What?"

"I got somebody sitting right here in your house," he said. "And she wants to buy it."

"Let me tell you something," I said. "If you're bullshitting with me right now, I'm gonna kick your ass."

"No, Viv," he said, speaking in a calm, pleasant voice that did not let the buyer know for one second that he was talking to a sleep-deprived lunatic. "She's about to go to the bank and make a down payment."

I sat right up in that bed. "Sold!" I said. "Sold!"

When I got back from China, I wanted to end things with my husband as swiftly and amicably as possible. I told him I had set up a fully furnished apartment and paid the rent for the year. I also put $50,000 in the bank for him. And I was done. **I didn't hate the guy. I just didn't want to be his wife anymore.**

When I left that house, it was like *Escape from Alcatraz*. I got a giant U-Haul and a bunch of my friends came over and helped me pack up my stuff. When the house was empty, we stood together, and they pledged that they would see me through this change. Then a couple too many of us squeezed into the front of the U-Haul. I was at the wheel, trying to be strong and keep it light for everyone, but I just started crying.

I was taking these huge gulps of air, and one of my friends touched my arm, saying, "Oh, baby," and probably thinking, *Oh, baby, don't you drive off this here road and get us killed!*

When I could speak, I said, "I'm free." I am so grateful for their love and support.

I made a *huge* profit selling that house, and I was now grown-up enough not to need another giant house to show people—or me—that I was a success. *See there*, I said to myself as we drove. *You buckled down and you figured it out. You let go.* Since then I've sold four houses, and I'm so proud of how well I've done. Real estate has been very good to me, and I highly recommend it as an investment. It's a cliché, but it's true: Let your money work *for* you, not against you.

Looking back, I have to take responsibility for this: When I let him move in after four months, I started a sprint to win that ring. Once I was engaged, I got wrapped up in planning that wedding.

I see young girls still doing this today, but I think it's changing. I love watching them graduating, getting their degrees, and pursuing their dreams. I get asked if I have any marriage advice for young women. The first thing I tell them is to get a prenup. I had one, thankfully. Of course, I think there is nothing wrong with having a bank account with your spouse, but do me a favor and keep a little bank account on the side. Just in case he or she gets a little crazy—it happens—you can say, "Okay, you can lose your damn mind by yourself. Because I love me some me."

But the main thing is to take your time and get to know your partner, and yourself, before you rush into making a commitment before God and the IRS.

And don't hold on to stuff too tightly that you squeeze the fun out of it. In life, I travel a lot lighter now. I recently finished a project and realized I had six days to myself. When I have that time, it means I declutter. It's not just that I am a neat freak. I am, but I just don't want to hold on to stuff that could mean more to someone else. Goodwill does very well when I get in a purge mode, and I also resell my expensive designer clothes on eBay and through the Real Real, an online luxury consignment shop. And there are few things I like more than calling some girlfriends and saying, "Vivica's garage sale is open, take what you want."

Do you have some purging to do? Think for a moment about your skinny clothes. The ones taking up room in your closet or in your drawer. Each day you see them, and each day they're taking up space. Let them go. Sell them online or at a consignment shop. Give them to the needy and the skinny, because they are just getting in your way.

Don't hold on to stuff that isn't working, whether it's a house you can't afford or a relationship you shouldn't invest more time in. I promise you, if something you thought would make you happy has become a burden, you are better off letting it go. Sometimes you'll make a profit, and sometimes you'll just cut your losses. But you'll be free.

THE DEVIL IS FINE, AND THAT'S HOW HE GETS YOU

For years, I took the high road with him. In my own twisted way, I was being true to the man I knew Curtis wanted to be.

I actually had no intention of even mentioning his name here. When I talked about this book with the publisher, he didn't even come up. I guess I was afraid that if I mentioned him, he would take credit for this, too. He'd say I sold a book on his name. Yet when Curtis has been on TV, in his 50 Cent role, he has made up stories about me and repeated them and got a reaction.

I see the comments his followers leave on my Instagram sometimes. I admit I can't help but click their profiles, and they're usually about sixteen with as many followers. Little boys who probably got their feelings hurt by a girl.

I keep getting dragged on back like it's *Indiana Jones and the Temple of Doomed Love*. Well then, let me put on my archaeologist hat and go back in to end this foolishness once and for all so we can all move on. Because there might be a lesson in there for you. I know there was one for me.

"Who's 50 Cent?"

It was early 2003, and I was sitting with one of my girlfriends, KimStacy Carter. Kim was reading a magazine, and had just told me, "You should date this guy 50 Cent."

She turned the magazine my way to show me the review of his *Get Rich or Die Tryin'*. The album cover had him shirtless, wearing a Louis Vuitton–patterned gun holster.

"He's hot," she said.

"Enhh, why's he got all that grease on him?" I asked.

"To show all those muscles."

"Not my type," I said.

His song "In da Club" was everywhere, so I kept hearing his name. But I swear he wasn't on my radar at all that spring. In June I was invited to the BET Awards, and I wore a short purple dress with a low cut and coral accents. I had my *Kill Bill* body and I wanted to show it off.

The photographers kept asking me for more photos on the carpet—*just saying*—so by the time I got into the theater the show was beginning. And there was that 50 Cent guy onstage, opening the show. I'd brought my makeup artist friend Tysula, and we were kind of cutting through the audience to get to our seats. As a fellow performer, I worried that this appeared rude. So I turned my head to look at him directly as I sidled to my seat.

And he stopped. It was this moment where he just got stuck. His boy onstage had to tap him, like, "Come on." And he went right back into the performance. Tysula and I sat down to watch him.

But it felt like he was watching *me*.

"Does it feel like he's looking at me?" I murmured to Tysula through a closed smile.

"Um, yeah," she said.

Later, when he went back onstage to accept the Best New Artist award, he leaned on the podium and looked right at me. "And I want to thank Vivica Fox for wearing that dress."

The camera panned to me and my look of shock. Well, I *was* shocked. I was there minding my own business. But, yes, I was flattered. I just didn't know what I was about to get into.

After that public display of flirting, I didn't hear a single word from him until a month later. It was around my thirty-ninth birthday in July and a van rolled up to my house. Two men came to the door, each holding a huge bouquet of lilies. They were my favorite, white Casa Blanca lilies.

"We have a flower delivery for Vivica Fox," one said.

"Come on in," I said. I started to talk about where they should put the flowers in my living room when one delivery guy politely stopped me.

"Ma'am," he said, "there's a lot more."

"It's the whole van," said the other guy.

In and out they went until the house looked like a florist. Everywhere I looked, there were white petals with dots of the gorgeous red stamens.

"Who sent them?" I asked.

"We're not supposed to say, ma'am."

Finally, they were done and I tipped them for their marathon delivery. Not five minutes after they left, my phone rang. It was my girlfriend Terry Christanio.

"50 Cent would like to speak with you."

"Okay," I said.

There was a pause and then a bashful, thick-tongued voice came on the line.

"Happy Birthday," he said.

"Thank you."

"Do you like the flowers?"

"This was you?" I screamed. "Oh my God, they're gorgeous. They're my favorite."

"I know," he said.

"How?"

"I asked around."

I later found out that he'd had his assistant reach out to Terry. While I was talking to Curtis, I leaned back on my white couch, bobbing my knee up and down like I was back in Indiana on the phone with a boy.

"Listen, where are you?" I asked.

"On tour."

"Oh, okay," I said. "Well, let me give you my private number so next time you just can call me."

"Sure."

"And what do I call you?"

"Just call me Curtis."

For the next month, Curtis and I were always on the phone while he was on tour. The calls started kind of slow, and then it was morning, noon, and always before he went to sleep. Sometimes he would be talking to me just as he was about to perform. I could hear a tech say, "All right, come to stage," and then I could actually hear the audience's screams. "Okay, baby," he'd say, "I'll call you after the show."

Especially those times, hearing the crowds cheer, I was amazed. "He is a *rock star*!" 50 Cent was blowing up, and Curtis was taking the time to share it with me.

Our conversations would usually go for an hour, sometimes longer. He was very proud of his son Marquise from a previous relationship with his ex Shaniqua Tompkins. Marquise was six and idolized his dad. Curtis also talked to me about his dreams, and what it was like to meet his heroes. We talked about my friend Tupac, who put me in one of his videos. And he talked about Biggie singing, "Watch me set it off like Vivica" in "What's Beef?" Yes, there were eleven years between us, but at twenty-eight he seemed to have the same work ethic I do. We got each other. I told my friend Lita Richardson, "I found a worker bee like me."

One time I asked him if touring made him miss things. Did he ever want to just go home?

"To what?" he said. "I worked so hard to get out of Queens. But you know what I'd like?"

"What?"

"We gotta figure out when you can come see me."

We did. He invited me to his show in Atlanta. "Bring a friend," he said. "I don't want you to have to come alone." So it was me and my girl Terry Christanio, who also did my hair and makeup. He flew us on a red-eye—first class, of course. Everything was always first class with Curtis. When I got to the airport, a limo waited to take me to the hotel. It felt like we were going to a premiere.

As we started driving, the driver lowered the partition.

"I'll be on standby for you during your stay, Miss Fox. Anywhere you want to go, I'll take you."

When the driver raised the partition, my friend Terry gave me a look. "Okay," she said, "I see 50 Cent is coming with his A game."

Truth be told, I was playing it cool for my friend, acting like I didn't care. Curtis was going all out courting me, and I had never been wooed like this before. Never.

Once I was in my hotel room, I kept standing up and sitting down, knowing he was going to come see me at any minute. We'd only ever talked on the phone. What if it was awkward in person? What if his breath reeked—please God, no—or what if he had some idea of Vivica A. Fox that was not me?

When he knocked on the door, I slipped into actress confidence. It's a bluffing trick you can use when you're nervous. I walked over in full Elizabeth Taylor grace, opened the door, and lifted my head to look him in the eye . . .

. . . and I melted. Bluff over. Curtis has the most beautiful eyes. You think the devil's ugly? Unh-unh. The devil is fine, and that's how he gets you. Curtis was six foot, wearing a doo-rag under his Yankees cap, and what I later found out was his best jersey. He was all muscle and smile.

He hugged me, and I just kind of fell into his incredible body. I looked up, and he kissed me. I was knocked out. TKO. I think I laid in bed with him the whole damn day, tracing my finger along the tattoos on his back, reading SOUTHSIDE and 50. He teased me about the little fox tat on my left arm, which I got at Shamrock Social Club on Sunset when I turned thirty.

"I was born a fox," I told him. "I'm gonna die a fox. That's my reminder."

We could talk about anything on the phone, and I was relieved that connection continued in real life. He was the nicest guy, just so sweet. He shared how long he had wanted for all of this to be happening to him. And it was happening.

As we talked in bed, I could also see scars from when he was shot nine times. The story went that he was in a car outside his grandmother's house when a guy snuck up and shot him point-blank. His hip, his calf, his hand, his pretty face . . . The story was part of his PR blitz, so of course I knew about it. He still had a bit of shrapnel trapped on the left side of his tongue, which changed his voice. But something told me he didn't want to talk about it, and in the coming months I would see how much fear he still lived with. Security was a constant concern of his. He had a bulletproof Suburban with a driver trained in defensive tactics. And he always seemed to have about six bodyguards hanging around in public and at least one guy outside his hotel room.

So naturally, that night he arranged a police escort to take us to the show. He put Terry and me in this little VIP area, and I noticed people clocking me, like, "What is she doing here?" But this was before social media and people tweeting, "Vivica Fox is in the next stall!"

When he first came out onstage, his big entrance was jumping off this New York skyline set they made. And he kind of tripped up on the landing. I screamed like any fangirl, wanting to cheer him on. By then I knew the words to his rhymes, and spat out the lines right along with him. Afterward, he was like, "I can't believe I slipped!" I made him nervous.

We had amazing chemistry, with fireworks going off in the room, absolutely. We were connected, but he wasn't one of those guys who wanted to screw all day. He was really focused on his success. Most of the time, I would be the one initiating sex because I really enjoyed making love with him. That's what made his later nonsense about me being a *Fifty Shades* dominatrix manhandling him so upsetting. We were vulnerable with each other, and our lovemaking was special to me.

When I left him after the concert, we went back to talking nonstop on the phone. One day in August, he said, "Hey, will you go to the MTV Awards with me?"

It felt like he was asking me to prom. He even sounded nervous.

"Of course I will," I said.

This would be our public debut as a couple, and I knew I had to bring it.

Let me tell you the story of The Dress.

I had been doing a lot of work with Randi Rahm, a fun, gifted designer from New York who believes in collaboration. When I created looks with her, I felt heard, but she also brought her own wow factor to the game.

I told Randi I needed a look, and confided that I had a feeling it would get a lot of attention because of Curtis.

"Please let me do this for you, Vivica," Randi said. "I want it to be special."

I put myself in her hands. Curtis and I decided we wanted to match colors—it really was like prom—and we decided on gray. I like to dress to a theme, so I told Randi I wanted something kind of rock and roll, and definitely edgy. I watched her brain work and could see genius take fire.

I like Randi because she's a hustler. Game recognizes game, right? She's a self-made, self-taught mom who at the time was just breaking into designing for celebrities. She sketched out a thigh-high mini, with sort of gladiator straps just covering my breasts. The drawing made me look like a superhero.

When I tried it on for the first fitting, I turned to check out my look in a full-length mirror. "Hell yeah, bitch," I said. "You look good."

Curtis knew that Randi and I were planning to knock it out of the park, and he wanted to keep up.

"What do you want me to wear?" he asked.

"Would you mind wearing a suit?" I asked. I just thought he would look so handsome in a nice suit.

"Not at all, I love wearing a suit," he said. "What about a hat? Is a hat too much?"

"Go for it, baby," I said.

In late August, I made the trip for the MTV Awards. Curtis flew me, Terry, and my go-to girl Lita to New York and put us up at the Four Seasons hotel. It was another red-eye, and when we got to the hotel that morning, Terry kept asking me a ton of questions. She continually stopped me from walking, asking me all this logistical stuff.

It was getting on my goddamned nerves. From the lobby to the elevator up to our floor, she kept yammering to me when all I wanted to do was get to my suite.

We exited the elevator and turned the corner. Just as I was about to tell her ass to stop already, I saw the first rose petal.

And another.

And another.

When I opened the door to my suite, there was a river of rose petals leading back to the bedroom. There were dozens of bouquets on every table and nightstand, every available surface. Roses by the bathtub, *in* the bathtub, and around the bed. I'd never seen so many in my life.

"Yeah," said Terry sheepishly. "I was talking so much to stall you. He wanted to surprise you."

Ding-dong. It was Curtis at the door. I just ran and jumped into his arms. He was so romantic and so charming. And the relationship was still *our* secret.

"Where do you want to have dinner tonight?" he asked.

"Maybe Mr. Chow's?" I knew it was nearby and it had an old-world classic ambience. It's a Chinese restaurant, with lacquered black-and-white surfaces and pops of red. Old-school waiters in white tuxedos that make you think of *Scarface* and Mafia movies. I knew Curtis loved those films, so I thought he would like dinner there. The Gangster and his Showgirl. Yeah, baby, it was on.

It was about four blocks from the hotel and I thought we'd just walk there, but that wasn't Curtis. He needed to be driven in his bulletproof car, nicer than the one I was in earlier. I got in the back with him, and there were all these cameras. Foolish me, I thought they were TVs. They were for security. Despite all the bodyguards I'd seen, that was the first time that I kind of thought, *Oh man, I've gotta be on my p's and q's with this guy.*

So when he arranged for us to have dinner in a private room at

Mr. Chow's, it was in a way romantic, but it was also for his sense of protection. When he took me out, he would often shut down restaurants for our dinners or get a secret room with security always nearby.

Curtis didn't like the food at Mr. Chow's. He was more of a cheeseburger-and-french-fries type of dude than a pot-stickers-and-Peking-duck kind of guy. But he'd found out all my favorite dishes and they just kept coming.

Near the end of the meal, this waiter walked in with a huge covered silver platter.

"Curtis, I can't eat any more," I said.

"Hold on," he said. "I have a surprise for you."

As the waiter lifted the lid, there was a platinum Rolex watch for me. Curtis took it and placed it on my left wrist.

Wait, he wasn't done.

When the car took us back to the hotel, three horse-and-carriage buggies were waiting outside the Four Seasons. We got in the middle carriage, and his security flanked us in the front and back carriages. He took me around Central Park, and we talked more about our dreams. We knew that by this time the next night, everyone would know about us.

"You were my dream girl, you know," he said.

"Really?"

"Yup," he said. "I used to watch *Two Can Play That Game* and *Set It Off* all the time. I mean, all the time." So much so that when his baby mama Shaniqua came home and found him watching the TV, she would say, "Are you watching that damn Vivica Fox *again*?"

"She laughed at me," he said. "She told me, 'A girl like that would never be attracted to you. Keep dreaming.'"

Oh God, but I was *so* attracted to him.

"I've always wanted to be in a power couple," he said. "Like Puffy and J.Lo. Or Will and Jada."

I put my head on his shoulder. Curtis was going to let me be me, I thought. Here was a man who wanted a union of equals. I wasn't gonna be just some trophy, at his disposal.

God, I was so naïve.

The day of the MTV Awards, Randi was getting me ready in my suite at the Four Seasons. It was an amazing moment when Curtis turned a corner and saw me for the first time.

"Wow," he said.

"It's all right?"

"Wow," he said again.

"Yeah, I look good, don't I?"

The photographers sure let me know. In the pictures I look a little scared at first. There was this whoosh of attention as every camera fired on us. Yeah, it was our coming-out moment, but I was kind of afraid it would be my coming-out-of-my-*dress* moment.

We were brought to our spot in the front row, and Eminem was seated next to us. He leaned in to whisper to me.

"Goddamn, you are wearing that dress," Eminem said.

All the attention made me a little self-conscious. I remember Madonna was sitting right behind me, and I so wanted to turn around and say, "I freaking love you." But I didn't, because I was thinking, *Okay, be cool, Vivica.*

But I damn near lost it when Beyoncé performed. I was not going to play it cool and let baby girl feel anything less than adored. She came down from the ceiling hanging by her feet, and then did a medley of "Baby Boy" and "Crazy in Love." When Beyoncé was done, I was jumping up and down so much—I can't even call it a *standing* ovation—that Bey gave me such a look of appreciation, like, "Thanks, Vivica."

The next morning, we found out we had shocked the world. Curtis and I were in bed together flipping between *Good Morning America*

e *Today* show. It was news! Britney Spears and Madonna had
onstage, and the other news angle was "GUESS WHO IS
ЕTHER?!"

hat dress was everywhere. People were like, "*Baaaby.*" I called my
ther and asked her what she thought of my dress.

"It could have used a little more fabric," she said.

We were in New York a few more days, and I had a bunch of photo
shoots lined up. The morning after the awards, I was shooting the
cover of *Today's Black Woman* magazine. It was going to take all day,
and he planned to spend the time with his son. Curtis told me he
couldn't wait to surprise Marquise with some clothes and sneakers.

I was busy at the shoot when he hit me with a text: "Yo, she won't
let me see the baby."

I immediately called him.

"I don't understand," I said. "What happened?"

"*You* happened."

Shaniqua was jealous, he said. He'd landed his dream girl.

"Where are you?" he asked.

"Sweetheart, I'm at my photo shoot."

"Okaayy," he said, sounding annoyed. "Can I come see you?"

Curtis came to the shoot, and I actually really liked it. Finally he
was seeing the kind of stuff I did. I was laying it on thick with my
model poses, and it lightened his mood—so much so that the pho-
tographer asked Curtis if he wanted to get in a few shots.

He didn't hesitate. Just said, "Yeah!" and got in the picture. I was
told they would only use the pictures for some inside shots. It wouldn't
be the cover. And I believed that.

After that, Curtis left to start a tour in Europe. I started traveling a lot for work, too, as the buzz for *Kill Bill* was helping me land
jobs.

Our schedules didn't match well for the level of phone calls he and

Vivica @ Age 3 + Ejuan.

ABOVE LEFT: Yes, that's me in plaid, hanging in my driveway with my neighbor Ejuan. She lived right behind me.

ABOVE RIGHT: Mugging for the camera with my cousin Dana (left) and her little brother, Devon.

LEFT: After church in front of my childhood home in Indy. I'm fifteen and holding my beloved nephew Devon (my brother Sandy's son). Mom is looking on in white, while Sugie stands so beautiful next to her late husband, Goldie.

BELOW: Mom standing by my brother Marvin and me. The woman in yellow is my mother's best friend, the late Fannie Dodd.

LEFT: An early modeling shot. I was so determined.

BELOW: Visiting from California at nineteen! Back with Ejuan and probably thinking I'm all that.

Vivica + friend
19 y. old

I loved working with Will Smith on *Independence Day*. I was so lucky to have a friend beside me for my big break.

With friends at the *Set It Off* after-party.

LEFT: With my *Why Do Fools Fall in Love* costar Lela Rochon Fuqua.

BELOW: Sharing a laugh with (from left) the late Dick Gregory, Rep. Maxine Waters, and Rep. John Conyers, who introduced me to the world of politics.

My *Booty Call* crew (from left): Tommy Davidson; our late director, Jeff Pollack; Jamie Foxx; and Tamala Jones.

Girls' day with Tichina Arnold, Tamala Jones, Elise Neal, and Tasha Smith.

LEFT: With the legendary Sidney Poitier.

BELOW: The Fox kids (from left): Marvin, Sug, Sandy, and me, showing love to Mom.

ABOVE: With my cutie-pie godson Christian after my L.A. show *Two Can Play That Game: The Stageplay.*

LEFT: My dad and his former wife Arlena at my wedding.

ABOVE LEFT: My business partner Lita Richardson and me on the *Kill Bill* set.

LEFT: With my amazing *Kill Bill* director, Quentin Tarantino. PHOTO BY ALBERT L. ORTEGA

BELOW: On the set of Lifetime's *Missing* with my costar Louis Ferreira.

Curtis and me after we came out as a couple at the VMAs. That's my wingwoman Lita on the right, along with Terry Christanio, who introduced me to Curtis.

Lita and me in my trailer as we co-produced my comedy *The Salon* in Baltimore. I was so skinny from heartbreak over Curtis. And no, I don't know what was so special about that damn boot.

I stopped in to say hi at a preschool while in Trinidad for Carnival.

Chilling on the *Today* show with Chrissy Teigen and her pretty self.

Bringing a Versace look for Andy Cohen on *Watch What Happens Live*.

Working that phone backstage for *Independence Day: Resurgence* at CinemaCon in Vegas.

Honoring our *Independence Day* director, Roland Emmerich, as he got his star on the Walk of Fame. PHOTO BY JEFFREY MAYER

Visiting Wendy Williams with the sexy squad of *Vivica's Black Magic*. PHOTO BY BJ COLEMAN

Back at *Wendy* with Columbus Short. PHOTO BY BJ COLEMAN

Cookie and Candace on the set of *Empire*. I adore my TV sister Taraji P. Henson.
PHOTO COURTESY OF FOX

In Jenny Packham at President Obama's last White House
Correspondents' Dinner. I got that dress on sale for fifty percent
off and I'm looking like a million dollars! You *know* I love a deal.
PHOTO BY BJ COLEMAN

I were used to, and frankly he would often forget my schedule even after I sent him an itinerary. One time I had a long flight and he called me about ten or twelve times while I was in the air. When I landed, I saw all the messages and panicked that something was wrong. By then his concerns for his safety were my concerns, and I worried someone had tried to hurt him.

Curtis's voice messages started, "Hey, baby, I love you," and quickly devolved into "Why are you ignoring me?" and "Call me back." In the last message, he simply said: "Fuck off, I'm not calling you until the tour is over."

Here's the thing, part of being a ride-or-die chick is that I take direction well. If a man tells me he doesn't want me on his team, I'm out. So I was out. If he called me and apologized, that was one thing. But I wasn't going to beg someone to be with me.

A few days later, I got a call from a number I didn't know. I picked up, thinking it might be a job. It was, just not a job I wanted.

"Please talk to him, Vivica."

It was James, his assistant.

"He won't talk to nobody," James said. "He won't eat."

So I called him. I thought that's what I was supposed to do. He answered the phone in his put-on tough voice.

"Yo, what's up?"

"Sweetheart, what is the matter?" I asked.

"Why were you ignoring me?"

"Because I was on a *plane*?" I yelled. "I told you."

"Oh, snap. I'm sorry."

It is embarrassing how many times we did this dance. Curtis would misunderstand something, usually involving my work, and he would announce that I was trying to break up with him. I often felt like I was walking on eggshells, and had to go out of my way to be super supportive.

Inevitably he would invent some fight, stop talking to me, and then someone from his team would call me. It felt like I worked for them. And I know the rap group he had formed, G-Unit, deeply resented me distracting Curtis—and distracting attention from them. I watched some MTV interview with the whole group, and the reporter quickly asked Curtis about me. I saw one of the members—I won't name him—roll his eyes in the background. Like, "This bitch again."

Long distance wasn't working, so I was really touched when he invited me to come to Europe to attend the World Music Awards in Monte Carlo. It's this amazing event hosted by Albert II, Prince of Monaco. Curtis was set to win Best New Artist, and yet he wanted me to be part of it. It was really touching because he knew I was hurt that I was not invited to any premieres on the *Kill Bill* publicity leg in Europe. "This will be your European tour," he said.

One of the organizers of the event found out I was coming and reached out to me on behalf of Prince Albert. "Hey, we hear you're going to be attending," he said. "We were wondering if you would like to host the show." Mariah Carey was coming, and so was Pink. They wanted it to be special.

Okay, now if you're the audience in this horror movie, this is the moment I need you to yell at the screen, "Don't do it, Vivica! Don't do it!"

But I said yes. This is what Angie from Indy was thinking, I swear: *This is so great because now he won't have to pay for my flight.* I thought I was being a good girlfriend, saving him money. *This is what a power couple does*, I said to myself.

Say it again and louder so I can hear you all the way back in time: "Don't do it, Vivica."

What I failed to realize was that Curtis wanted this to be his night. Later I would realize I was insulting his manhood by standing equal with him.

———

Monte Carlo is one of the most beautiful places in the world, especially in October. It's a gorgeous little place set on cliffs looking over the Mediterranean, and when the temperature drops to the sixties at night, men lend their tuxedo jackets to women in gowns. It is like a film set of old Hollywood. The roads are winding and glamorous, the same ones that Monaco's Hollywood princess, Grace Kelly, drove with Cary Grant in *To Catch a Thief*.

There I was in this city of romance, and Curtis would not even talk to me. We didn't even share a room. I did what I always did when I needed help. I called my father. At first I pretended I was just calling to let him know I had landed safely. But then I got real. "Curtis won't talk to me," I said. "I don't even know where he's at."

Dad diagnosed the problem right away, more than four thousand miles away in Indiana. "Evidently he wanted to do this for *you*, Angie," he said. "This is his night and you were supposed to be his guest, not the host."

"Dad, I thought it would make him happy," I said.

"You can't charge right in there, baby. Don't always be doing. Sometimes you gotta be done for."

I closed my eyes and said an empty "I know." I looked out a window and sighed. "Daddy, I am in *Monte Carlo*," I said, starting to cry. "I'm supposed to be happy and I'm not."

"Just play it cool," he said. "He'll come around."

Dad was right. Curtis finally spoke to me. Even that seemed like a miracle. We made plans to meet in my hotel room, and then I made everything about a thousand times worse by trying to do an over-the-top gesture for him. I had my room filled with roses. The same way he had done for me at the Four Seasons.

When he walked in, he scanned the room and his face hardened into a sneer.

"Are you trying to compete with me?"

"What?" I said, honestly blindsided that he could think that. "I don't . . . I'm your partner. I wanted to do what you did for me."

"Forget it."

Forget it. That was his thanks.

But I am a trouper. I did that whole awards show, and I will tell you that I nailed it. When the show was over, there was so much energy backstage, with people high-fiving and yelling, "That was great!" Curtis and I just looked at each other. No words. I went to my dressing room and sat on a couch, leaning my head back. I was still in the white Randi Rahm fitted pantsuit I wore onstage. People had been around me all night, fussing over my hair and face, and here I was alone. I could stop smiling.

I felt him come in the dressing room. Before I even opened my eyes, I knew it was Curtis. He sat across from me on the couch, and we stared at each other for a little while. There had been so many times we had just looked into each other's eyes, but this time I didn't have a single clue what he was about to say.

"You did do good," he said.

"Thank you," I said. "It wasn't worth losing you."

"You didn't lose me," he said.

Honestly, at that point I was so afraid to say the wrong thing that I silenced myself. Here's what I wanted to say: "If this mattered to you so much, why didn't you tell me? Why do I have to guess about what I actually did wrong when you are always so ready to accuse me of something I didn't do?"

Instead, I hugged him and we kissed. I decided that if I just did as little as possible to set him off, he would stay the Curtis I knew.

We had one more night in Monte Carlo. A bunch of us went out to a restaurant, and Curtis was actually fun again. I thought, *We're back on track.* Later that night we were in bed and I kissed him. He pulled back and kind of put his lips in the little-boy pout position that always signaled trouble.

"You'll never love me like I love you," he said.

"What are you talking about?"

"I like you more than you like me."

He left the next morning, and I didn't know he was keeping a secret from me. I later found out that he had planned to propose on that trip to Monaco.

Curtis changed his mind after I took the hosting gig. His plan was to rent out a theater in Monte Carlo and show a print he had obtained of *Kill Bill*. We were going to watch it and at the end, he was going to ask me to marry him. He had a twelve-carat diamond engagement ring.

I didn't know any of this until about a year later. Instead of giving me the ring, he had the diamond broken in two. He wore them as earrings.

He had the ring.

When I found that out, it broke my heart all over again.

When we left Monaco, I had no idea what might have been. I came back to America and I started work on *The Salon* in Baltimore. I thought everything was fine, or at least as "fine" as I was now used to.

Then that issue of *Today's Black Woman* came out with the huge photo of us on the cover. I had been promised the images of Curtis and me would just be inside and not on the cover. The story was all about me, with him looking like a plus-one. I knew he wouldn't be happy. I called him right away and left a message saying I didn't know this was going to happen.

The next thing I know, my stylist friend Darryl Brown called.

"Yo, your boy's on the radio blasting you."

"Who?"

"50."

He was going on a rant. That was it. It was the beginning of him telling the world I was a fucking bitch. "She used me," he said. He was repeating the words of his boys, who had always been trying to convince him that he was whipped: "She used you for fame. You're on the cover of a girls' magazine. You're a pussy. You're a wimp." It was their way of getting me back for every time a reporter whooshed by them at an event to ask 50, "What's it like to date a movie star?" And for the Rolex I got that they thought they deserved. Instead of Curtis coming to me and us attacking this together as a couple, I became the enemy of 50 Cent.

He got such a reaction out of the first radio interview that it was like he was on the Stomp Vivica tour. He was on the radio daily, assassinating my character. The awful thing was that I was a feel-bad girl working on a feel-good dramedy. *The Salon* is about a smart hairdresser who owns her own place, but a big corporate company wants to buy up the neighborhood. I'd taken it because I wanted to be in a black ensemble film with a strong female lead who can take care of business and herself. And every day I was crying. All the damn time. I'd start crying in the makeup chair, and they would have to start doing my makeup again. I lost ten pounds because I was too sad to even eat. I look at that movie and see I was gaunt.

Kym Whitley was on the movie, and every day she would knock on my trailer door and check on me. She is so funny and so kind. She told me to stay strong. "He's just mad because he's in love with you."

Really? Because this just seemed like some Dr. Jekyll two-faced garbage. He started to up the ante changing his tune, saying I was stalking him. I was in Baltimore making a movie. I wasn't in his freaking bushes.

And then something in me said, *Push through. Push through.*

He stayed away and gradually stopped talking about me. Then I was in Vancouver working on a guest thing for a show. They put me up in a hotel, and while I was there, I decided to get a facial at the hotel's spa. The facialist worked my pores and even did the cucumber-slice thing on the eyes. I was so relaxed.

She left for a moment and then came back in.

"Uh, Miss Fox, you have a visitor."

"Who?" I asked. Who would even know I was here?

"50 Cent is here."

I took off one cucumber slice to look at her and see if this was some kind of joke.

"He came in here asking for you."

"You're really not kidding," I said.

"Would you like him to leave?"

I paused. "No," I said. "It's time for us to talk."

"He made us promise not to tell you," she said with the tiniest bit of fear in her voice. "Can you please act surprised when you walk out?"

Even she thought this was crazy. Well, I never got dressed so slowly. I wanted to make him wait, and maybe a small part of me hoped he'd give up and leave.

Finally, I went in the waiting room and there he sat, leaning forward in his chair. I stared at him for a long time, a whole range of emotions going over me. Love, hatred, that feeling of betrayal, but mainly love. *Dammit*, I thought, *you still love him.*

Meanwhile, he began to stand, and his face slowly changed to "Oh, damn, what is she going to do?"

I walked right over and hugged him.

"Why did you leave?" I asked quietly. "Why did you leave? Oh my God, why?"

"Let's just go somewhere private," he said. He was Curtis again. That voice I'd missed. "What room are you in?"

I took him upstairs and we hung out. I ordered room service and I got him his favorite: cheeseburger and fries. We turned on the TV and watched football. Like nothing had ever happened. And as Curtis stared at the screen, he was able to open up without looking at me. He told me how much pressure he was under, and how hard it was to date someone famous. He said his guys said dating me made him look soft. And image was everything in the rap game. He was sorry.

And I accepted it. I thought that was being a strong woman: You talked all that shit about me and now you're sorry? Look how strong I am. Look how loyal I am. Look what I am capable of being for you.

I know now that people do this all the time. You get with someone so toxic that loving them is a test of your strength and you will not allow yourself to fail. You think it's strong to hang in, but that's just what you tell yourself so you don't lose the person you love.

I say I know this now because I sure as heck didn't know it then. I just thought, *I'll follow his lead.*

So he started his reappearing act. There were more moments like the Vancouver spa. He showed up at my house, waiting for me to come home. I walked in to find him in my living room, playing with my cat Snookie. Finally, I just asked him: "What's going on?"

"I've just got to figure out how to handle this," he said. "I want to be with you."

But he didn't. If he meant it, he would have stood up to his silly friends with their "No Girls Allowed" rules. I never told anybody this, about all the times that he would show up. I never betrayed that confidence because I was still in love with him.

In 2009, he asked me to be in his video for "Do You Think About Me?" He told me he wanted to shock the world again, like we did at the MTV Awards. He wanted it to be majorly cinematic, with a whole story line. There were two female roles in the video. One was the new girl, and the other was a caricature of the "psycho ex," slashing tires, going crazy in front of the mirror. He thought it would be funny if I played the new girl. And fool me said, "I'll do this for you because I care about you, and I know it will get more attention for you if I play the crazy chick."

He paid me $25,000 to do the video, flew me to New York, and gave me a huge trailer. He greeted me in my trailer and thanked me. "You know you're my first wife," he said. "We just never actually got married."

My friend Tamala Jones from *Two Can Play That Game* played his new love interest, and she told me that Curtis spent the whole time saying he had done me wrong and he loved me. She told this to me like it was a revelation, but it was just more mind games. I noticed he had a lot of young guys around him, buzzing about. A new generation of boys telling him how to act.

Curtis went on another radio show, playing 50 Cent and talking about all the women who were supposedly after him just because he worked with them. "Wait till you see my next video," he said on the show. "What are they gonna say when they see Vivica Fox?" The DJs didn't believe him and asked why in the world I would do that since he had been so cruel to me. They even asked if we were having sex again, and he chose to play coy. "No, we weren't sexually active," he said, then paused. "At the video." He got the laughs he wanted.

He called me on New Year's 2010, but I didn't pick up. I was with someone else and had already decided I needed to move on. *That chapter of your life is over*, I told myself. I'd had a great love, and Curtis shrunk from that greatness. I was proud that I tried and that I believed in love. I didn't feel weak.

He had one more trick up his sleeve in his reappearing act. It was the May 2013 premiere of Will's movie with his son Jaden, *After Earth*. It was a family kind of night, and I was sitting in the theater feeling very happy to be part of the Smith extended family.

Someone tapped my shoulder and I turned.

It was Curtis. "What's up?"

I stood up and we hugged. Every headline about him had been drama lately, and he was staring at me so intensely. "Are you okay?" I asked.

"I'm all right," he said in a little-boy voice. "I'll call and I'll talk to you soon."

There was something concerning about it. "I'm serious," I said. "Let me know if you want to talk."

"I will," he said. "I'll find you."

Instead, he kept talking *about* me. Which was fine—I convinced myself I could take it. But then he went after my *Empire* family. I was cast in the second season of *Empire*, getting to work with my friends Taraji P. Henson, Terrence Howard, and Jussie Smollett. Being with them is like a family reunion. And they were also in Curtis's sights.

By then, Curtis had moved from radio dissing to using Instagram as his weapon of choice. I guess he felt *Empire* was eclipsing his Starz show, *Power,* and so he hit out against them a few times. On October 15, he reposted an Instagram saying *Empire*'s ratings had declined because of all "the gay stuff." (He later deleted it and sent his rep out to say he hadn't read the whole thing and missed the homophobia.) I was so sad because I suspected "the gay stuff" was code for Jussie Smollett, who came out in March 2015. I have known Jussie since he was seven years old, working with his five amazingly talented siblings. We used to hang out and eat french fries, talking about movies. The kids called themselves the von Trapps, but I remember them most as the first vegetarian family I knew. I love Jussie with all my heart. The antigay remarks really bothered me because here is someone working his ass off and it's dismissed out of sheer pettiness.

So in November 2015, Andy Cohen had me on *Watch What Happens Live.* We talked about me being on *Empire* for the second season, and he asked me what I thought about 50 Cent's comments about gay themes ruining the show. I went on autopilot and I let my anger do the talking. "First of all, you know, 'the pot called the kettle black' is all I'm saying," I said. "He's not," I continued. "I mean, we had a great time. He just seems like he's got something that's not quite clear." It was an incredibly clumsy way of saying it.

Well, that did it. I didn't hear from him directly, but he slammed me on his Instagram. "Oh No!!!, Now she thinks I'm gay because I let her lick my Ass. LMAO. Wait, I didn't want her to, she forced me, my hands were tied. 50 shades of grey."

Listen, I'm a grown-ass woman. If that was my kink and what I was into, then I would do it. Our lovemaking was so cherished and special to me that it hurt to see him make up stories. But he did get a reaction out of it. So of course he didn't stop.

Once my episodes aired, he went after my *Empire* family big-time. He posted a side-by-side of me and some poor woman with a misshapen face. "I don't know why people would want to cross me," he wrote. "I would stay out of my way, if I wasn't me because I'm gonna keep winning."

Taraji—an Oscar and Emmy nominee and Golden Globe winner, mind you—came to my defense with a comment on his post. "I prob should leave this alone but I despise bullies," she began, before suggesting that perhaps 50 should just be happy for others.

When he responded to Taraji, he told her he hoped she could eat her trophies. Jussie came right to the defense of Taraji and me, his on-screen mom and auntie, saying 50 should hold up women, not tear them down. "You're in your 40s brother. It's time to leave all childish, pettiness behind."

I had brought this to them. He was aiming for me, and he took on my *Empire* family to hurt me. Jussie, my french-fry-eating boy turned gorgeous leading man; Taraji, who I watched work for fifteen years to win success without sacrificing her principles; Terrence Howard, who I knew when we were starting out, talking about how we were going to make it. People who work so hard, freezing their asses off filming in Chicago to put out a hit show. People who defy all odds to be a black ensemble show that *everyone* wants to watch.

He could say what he wants about me, but not my family. I decided I would no longer protect him. When he went on *Watch What Happens Live* in December 2016 to spout more lies about me, I let him have it on my Instagram. The devil can only tempt me so much.

I thought it would just end with that note of anger, but the Lord intervened. I was in New York City to promote *Vivica's Black Magic* right after the 2017 New Year. I had a night off, so I decided I would take up Madison Square Garden's offer of courtside seats for the New York Knicks–Orlando Magic basketball game.

Right before we left the hotel, my friend and publicist BJ Coleman got a message.

"Okay, I gotta tell you something," he said.

"What?"

"50 is going to be there tonight."

"Really," I said. But then I thought about how I had been talking up this trip to New York on my social media. In his defense, he does love basketball almost as much as I do.

I looked in the mirror. I had my hair up, and I wore black leather jeans and a gray knit sweater. I completed the look with above-the-knee Michael Kors boots and a Helen Yarmak light fur to fend off the New York chill. I was glad I listened to one of my rules: **Always look good—you never know who you'll run into.**

My friend and I got to MSG early, where we were met by a lovely woman who was panicked about the double booking of me and 50 Cent. She kept apologizing. "Um, just so you know," she said, "you're on one end and he is on the other. You guys aren't by each other."

"Honestly," I said, "I am okay. Listen, I don't have a problem with him being here."

I went up to a small VIP area to kill time before the game and I was so excited because there was Cate Blanchett, with her handsome son. Curtis left my mind immediately. I fanned out, and decided I just had to say hi. She is so amazing, and has shown such versatility on the screen. She is a *star*, and that sometimes makes it hard for actresses. You run the risk of watching her work and saying, "There's Cate Blanchett playing Queen Elizabeth" or "Oh, there's that Cate Blanchett again, this time playing a 1950s lesbian." But she does a disappearing act on-screen, and surrenders herself to the role.

"I'm sorry to bother you," I said. She turned and I stuck out my hand. "I'm Vivica—"

"Vivica Fox!" she shouted with a smile.

You get so excited about people that you think they don't know you, and she did. I don't know if her son saw *Kill Bill* or *Independence Day* because he couldn't have been sweeter, too.

"I just love your fashion sense," I told her.

"Oh, honey, talk about fashion," she said, gesturing to me with her glass of Chardonnay. "Look at that coat."

It was such a vote of confidence. We were all brought to our seats, and my friend ordered a Maker's Mark, neat. I thought to myself, *Honey, you might need a bourbon for this.*

"Make it two," I said. "But put a lot of ice in mine."

It was an A-list night. Besides Cate, there was Ron Howard, Michael J. Fox, Matt Lauer . . . and there he was, Curtis. He came in wearing a green bomber jacket, tan-gray acid-washed jeans, and a white baseball cap.

Just as I practiced a face of "I see you, and I'm the coolest cucumber at the grocery," the jumbotron played a clip of *Independence Day: Resurgence.* Then the announcer said, "Ladies and gentlemen, welcome Vivica A. Fox!"

They went to a live shot of me. I had that drink in my hand, so I toasted everybody and said, "Happy New Year, darlings!" I was the first celebrity attendee up on the screen, so people were primed to cheer. I'm an L.A. girl, so to have that huge New York crowd cheering for me felt amazing.

At halftime we were brought up to the private lounge. The place looks like an elegant old cigar lounge, dark with gold accents. There are about ten tables with a few couches, and you sit there in an atmosphere of "good ol' money."

Cate walked by. "Hey, girl," she said.

"Hi there," I said.

I sat at my table with my friend BJ. "Oscar winner Cate Blanchett just hey-girl'ed me," I said. "Damn, hashtag life is good."

I spotted Curtis walking in with his little entourage. He took a table across the room, and the VIP lady came nervously over to me.

"He wasn't supposed to come up here," she said.

"Sweetheart, I am telling you, it's okay."

"I just . . ."

I was mortified that someone so kind and so good at her job was worried about something as trifling as adults who can't be in the same *arena* together.

"I tell you what," I said. "I'll prove it. I'm just going to go over and say hi."

Her eyes widened. Like she could hear the *ding-ding* at the start of a boxing match. This *was* MSG after all.

I stood up, smoothed my pants, and walked over.

Curtis looked up at me. And his face broke into a huge smile. That pretty, authentic smile I had loved when we first met. That smile melted my heart.

"Happy New Year," I said softly.

"Happy New Year," he said.

"Can I have a hug?"

"Of course," he said. He stood to hug me, then pulled me in to sit at his table. His boys looked like they didn't know what was going to happen. There was one with a black baseball cap.

"You've been bad," Curtis said.

He was referring to my Instagram. I wanted to take the bait, explain to him exactly why I had to go off on him. But I listened to my better angels. I just turned to everyone at his table. "This is family," I said. "Regardless of what we go through, we are family."

He took a long look at me. "Yep." He sighed. "First wife."

Baseball Cap guy fell back in his seat and took off his hat to wave his face. "Oh, thank God," he said. "I had no idea, Vivica. I had no idea what was gonna happen. Thank you, God. We're all good."

Curtis and I made small talk about our families for a minute, and I said I had to go.

"We need to stop this," I said.

"Yes," he said.

This was the fighting, but it was also the push and pull. By consistently reacting to him, I was only extending my grief. Enough.

As I walked back to my table, I let out a sigh. *That was the right thing to do*, I told myself. *Good girl.*

Whether I had been holding on to love or holding on to anger, I had to learn to let go. I was finally FREE.

STOP FALLING IN LOVE WITH A SIX-PACK AND A SMILE

As I write this, I am single. As your sister girl, I will not lie to you: I don't want to be single. But I'd rather be single and happy than be with someone and unhappy. I say "as I write this" because I have hope. I have asked the Lord for greater blessings than a man—my work, my family's health—and He has come through. So I have made a conscious effort to wait for my king to share the castle I have built. I am open to adjoining castles, too.

You know that I have had a reputation for taking in the young ones. A few years ago I had to make a conscious effort to stop falling in love with a six-pack and a smile. I joke that I used to date body parts. I also just got tired of being treated poorly. **When you're younger, you like the bad boys, but when you grow up, the bad boys just get on your nerves.**

When I am out with my girls, I always get the young guys coming up to me. A warning to all you powerful women who can buy your own drinks: If a guy approaches and has nothing to offer you but his youth, he is going to play the angle of taking you down a peg. Each thinks he is the player who invented the trick of acting disrespectful to get your attention. One guy asked me a question, and as I began to explain, he cut me off.

"Blah blah blah," he said. "Why don't you just answer my question?"

Excuse me?

"Okay, you're two seconds away from never talking to me again," I said. "And you better work on that tone." It was an immediate turn-off and I kicked him to the curb. If he is coming over here still smelling of Similac, then he best show some respect.

I met this one incredibly hot young guy recently, and I thought, *Maybe I should just screw him and have a fun night.* But I knew exactly how this movie would play. Same script, different lead actor. My girl-friends are so funny. "Do the maintenance," they say. "You need that maintenance sex to keep everything running smoothly."

Trust me, in my day, I had a whole lot of maintenance going on. But now I feel that sharing yourself with someone is more than just an act. If I allow someone in my space and in my spirit as I share my body with that man, it's got to mean something.

This shift in my thinking happened after I ended an engagement to a younger man in 2011. My last six-pack and a smile. I knew for a while we weren't going to work out, but I still felt I had to go through with the wedding. My sister, Sug, was one of the only people I confided in. I told her flat-out that I felt trapped.

"Oh God, what am I gonna do," I said. "And what are people gonna say?"

"You're miserable," she said.

"But I got the dress." This seemed important at the time.

"Stop it, Angie," she said. "Don't do this."

She saved me. I'd fallen for that peer pressure again and said I was gonna get married. I thought I had to go through with it. *A deal's a deal*, I thought. Sug gave me the strength to walk a different path.

For once, I decided to take a break from jumping from relationship to relationship. First I had to find out if it was even okay for me to be alone. Even though I've been on my own since I was seventeen, still as a girl I was always saying, "I want to have a boyfriend," or I would find someone to make out with for my ego: "Look who I'm messing around with, everybody!"

Now I decided I was going to date me for a while. Treat myself and share my success with me for a bit instead of seeing my riches light up someone else's life. I remember standing in the mirror, smoothing my dress, and saying, "Where am I at?"

So I did the work of examining myself. **I looked at all my failed relationships and realized that the common denominator was me.** I also saw other patterns. Like my obsessive need to be self-reliant. I have always been determined to be my own provider. I like having my own stuff. Like my mother, I don't want anyone holding anything over my head. My worst nightmare is some man saying, "You know I gave that to you . . ." No, you didn't.

So I unconsciously chose men who were in absolutely no danger of providing for me. I inherited my mother's work ethic, but she also—inadvertently and directly—taught me to approach relationships from a place of wariness. Not only have I been afraid to give up control and thus have the rug pulled out from under me, I have simply been fearful of heartbreak. My father hung the moon for me, but it is a true fact that he was my mother's first love and she never, ever got over him.

I have watched my mother carry that all my life, so I have a severe freaking allergy to feeling disappointed in someone. I've stayed guarded with men so it wouldn't happen to me. The second that I am close to feeling too much and risking getting hurt like my mother, I start booking flights to get the hell out of there.

As I resolve to wait until the right man comes along, I have to acknowledge that it's tough out there, isn't it? Guys, you've gotten spoiled. You used to court us girls. Now girls are running after guys instead of letting men earn us. In the wild, when the animal wants to get the female's attention, he does all his tricks. The peacock gets up and shows some feathers. The gorilla beats his chest. Nowadays, all the guys need is a wallet and the girls go crazy. These guys nowadays are so lazy that they forget to romance you.

I had this email thing going with a guy I met on a plane. It seemed promising. We met when we were seated next to each other. What caught my eye? First of all, it was a brother flying in first class with no ring on his finger. Let's just say that kind of thing stands out. He was tall and had a great smile. And he seemed like a real man, not some overgrown boy.

He didn't recognize me at first. When I travel, I wear a baseball cap and no makeup. We started talking about traveling, and I mentioned that I was going to see my nephew who just joined the military . . .

"Oh, I used to be in the military," he said.

That broke the ice, so I talked more, thanking him for his service. He paused for a minute.

"Are you Vivica Fox?"

"Yeah."

"Oh, wow."

It let us connect as human beings. People expect me to be Vivica Fox all the time, and it seemed like we got past that right quick. When we landed, he asked if I wanted help with my carry-on. I flashed on something I was told at a women's conference I attended in London. This woman got up there and said, "I had to learn to be a little bit more submissive." I will tell you that my initial response was "Screw you." But she said to just try to let men help me. So I said to myself, *Just try, Vivica.*

"Thank you," I said. "That would be nice."

He then had a guy bring all my luggage to my car, had it loaded up, and then tipped the guy. He was a gentleman.

"I'd like to stay in touch," he said.

I gave him my email, because the phone just seemed too personal. Usually I'd jump in the shallow end headfirst. "Here's my number," I'd say. "Come! Stay with me! Be with me!" Nope. I made that promise to myself not to do that anymore.

It went okay. I got excited when I saw his name in my in-box. It gave me butterflies, and for me if I don't have instant butterflies— that little "Oooh"—it's not interesting. But you have to stay vigilant. Because guys, when they want something from you, they can BS you to get to it. **You can date someone for months and then all of a sudden you meet the real guy.** "There you are," you say. "I thought you'd be coming. And there you are."

He was emailing me on the regular, but then he disappeared over Thanksgiving weekend. Four days, nothing. He said he lost his phone. Now, when a man leaves the house, he has his wallet, his keys, and his phone. He forgets his wallet, he'll get by. Forgets his keys, he'll find a way in. But his phone? The man will march right on back and get that phone. So it was suspect that he didn't get a replacement, but also weird that he didn't just get on a computer to email me.

He didn't really get why I thought it was a little rude and suspect to go from emailing me twice a day to nothing at all.

Here's the deal: If you are a grown-ass person like me, you don't want to get entangled in the loose ends that your potential boyfriend or girlfriend has not tied up. I love my sisters way too much to get in the middle of anything, and I cannot have someone putting me at risk for getting blasted on social media: "Vivica Fox is trying to ruin my marriage." Nope.

I was born at night, but not last night.

So many girls tell me the same thing: "I can't meet a quality guy." I was in Houston a couple of weekends ago for a women's expo. I did a motivational speech, and during the Q&A, this young lady stood up and right away she asked me for dating advice.

"Well, what type of man are you looking for?" I asked.

She was ready with a whole checklist, right down to salary requirements. He had to be fit, no kids, career-driven, handsome.

"So you want Prince Charming," I said.

"Yes!" she said.

"Then let me ask you this," I said. "What are *you* doing to meet this man? Because it sounds to me like you're waiting for this guy to just come and find you. That's not gonna happen."

There was a police officer standing near me for security, a gorgeous black man, and I could tell he was listening intently.

"You gotta learn to go to different places to meet different kind of men," I continued. "Go to the environments where the type of man you say you want actually congregate."

"Like a bar?" she asked.

"Think more strategically," I said. "You don't want to be at a bar where a bunch of finance dudes are standing around getting drunk with each other. You might hook up with one of them, but that's not going anywhere."

She looked confused, so I broke it down. "This man you want to meet?" I said. "He golfs. He plays tennis. He's in a running club."

I could see the light turning on her head. She had this cardboard cutout of a guy in her head just showing up—his life beginning when he saw her face. It never occurred to her that he might actually be out there, you know, living his life and not hopelessly searching for her!

"I should take golf lessons then," she said.

"Look, you won't be the first person to realize that successful men golf," I replied. "So don't bother with the silly lessons or sailing classes unless you really want to learn. It will be all women looking for men, trust me. Sign up for a cute little fun run. Or check out the driving range. A bucket of balls will cost you at most ten dollars. A small investment can have a big return."

"I can do that," she said.

I noticed the police officer do a quick nod in agreement.

"Yes, you can," I said. "But seriously, just try going to a really fabulous restaurant on your own and buy yourself a drink at the bar. Dress up like you would for a first date with this person you have in mind, and don't show up looking like the thirst trap. Guys are gonna notice. And if you notice an attractive man doesn't have a ring and he's by himself, why don't you offer to buy him a drink? Don't wait for a man to do something. If you are interested in someone, ask *him* to dinner."

The police officer couldn't take it and had to join in. "That's good advice, Vivica!" he said. "That would get my attention."

It would get *any* man's attention, so just choose what man you want. This young woman put an emphasis on the guy's bank account, so I tailored the advice to her. But if you're saying, "Oh God, I don't care how much he makes, I'm just tired of meeting jerks," well then, think about where nice, civic-minded guys congregate. They volunteer for charities. They get involved in political campaigns and initiatives.

This isn't about becoming someone you're not just to meet a man. You can't pretend to be a golf fan or feign passion for a local cause if your heart isn't in it. But looking into these experiences will give you a better sense of what attracts the men that *you* want to attract.

I gave that young woman in Houston one last piece of advice, which I will share with you. Get your face out of your damn phone. Look around and pay attention. When you are staring at a phone because you want to kill time or not appear awkward in public, you are telling any and all potential partners that whatever is on that phone deserves more attention than them. Do you want to miss out on a spontaneous connection because you were half reading some inspirational meme about getting what you want in life?

That guy I met in first class was at least a grown-up, so I feel I'm on the right track. **I find a lot of my girlfriends are unlucky in love because they date the same man over and over again.** Each time they think, *Now, this one I can change!* But you can't force people to be who they're not meant to be. If you think you can train a man to be nicer to you, you're dreaming. Find you a gentleman and don't waste time with him.

So what's your six-pack? Think about the guys you've dated or the guys you've pursued if you've been unlucky in love. Answer these questions for each guy:

Name:
The draw:
The pluses:
The minuses:
What I tried to change about him:
Time I knew it was over:
Time it actually ended:

Now look at it all together. There's valuable information here. The draw tells you what you were looking for. If we're being honest, the answers will sometimes be "I needed to have a boyfriend to feel successful," or "He was hot," or even "He asked me out."

The pluses are obviously the good qualities. They can be superficial, like "He was sexy," or deep, "He wanted kids." The minuses are what we now know we need to avoid in the future.

My favorite is looking at what you tried to change about him. If you are the type to date fixer-uppers, this is where we get into it. I've been with mean men who I thought I could turn into gentlemen. I have girlfriends who date cheaters time and again, and think they are going to magically cure them. The person you wanted to change him into is the person you should have been looking for in the first place.

And then we look at time. This is about trusting our instincts and not wasting time. Because you know when it's over, but that doesn't mean you stop trying. It can be sobering to look at the length of time between when you realized this wouldn't end well and when you or the other person actually did something about it. *Years* can go by, years that you could have been happy.

It's hard to break that cycle and risk going it alone. Don't get me wrong, I still get butterflies. If I didn't, I'd be dead. My crushes run all the colors of the rainbow, and they're fun to have. But I don't want to settle.

I can see the pros and cons to living alone. I wake up every day and can do whatever I want. But some days, like today, I wake up and I would like somebody here to share God's blessings with. So I wait.

PART FOUR

LOOK
AMAZING
AT ANY AGE
OR BUDGET

DRESS FOR THE LIFE YOU DESERVE

I was doing an interview with Tracey Edmonds on *Extra* a little while back, rocking this really cool St. John Knits military jacket with my own jeans. Tracey told me she loved my Jimmy Choo booties.

"Who's your stylist?" she asked.

"Oh, her name is Vivica Fox," I said, laughing. "Write that down because I think she is going places. V-I-V-I-C-A . . ."

It's true. I love to shop, and I'm not paying a stylist to have all that fun. I know what works for my body and I know value. I began honing my shopping prowess when I started out as an actress. I *had* to shop smart: My budget was near zero. So in between premieres and fancy dinners, I would hit Goodwill and scour consignment shops. I became a bona fide expert in hunting down very gently used designer clothes. When you hear an actress on the red carpet say she is wearing "vintage," it doesn't necessarily mean she picked it out of Coco Chanel's temperature-controlled couture walk-in hope chest. It just means *someone* wore it before her. Julia Roberts and Penelope

Cruz went up to the stage to accept their Oscars wearing used Valentino and Balmain, respectively. They killed it!

I needed to find designer labels not out of a sense of vanity, but because early on I figured out how the red carpet game worked. At first, I would buy something from Bebe that I thought was pretty. And I'd get all dressed up, pose for a million photos, and talk to every reporter on that press line. Then I would look at the weeklies and there would be no me. I would be like, *But I thought that was cute?!*

It was cute, but it wasn't a cute enough *tag*. It's a business and I had to learn the rules. Big designers take out expensive ads in these magazines. When I wore one of the big guns—a Gucci or a Calvin Klein—the designer names would catch the eyes of magazine editors. They'd then run my photo with a caption reading something like, "Vivica A. Fox, in Gucci, attended the May 19 premiere at Mann's Chinese Theater." And a few pages later, look at that giant gorgeous Gucci ad. They are called "fashion credits" for a reason. That coverage was so important when I was starting out, because every casting director read those magazines looking for new faces. Can't win the game if you don't play.

I'll never forget the first time *and only time* I ended up on a worst-dressed list in a magazine. It was so humbling, to be honest with you. You know the movie *Carrie* when she goes to the dance and they all laugh at her? Yeah, it kind of felt like that.

It was June of 1997, and this was before I was sure of my look and what works for me. I was attending the Atlanta premiere of *Batman & Robin* for Warner Bros. In the movie I play Ms. B. Haven, a henchwoman of Arnold Schwarzenegger's Mr. Freeze. It was a campy, cartoony film, and I let a stylist talk me into this fool outfit. It was a blue-tinged mixture of a sheer top with a band across the boobs made out of another material, sheer across the stomach, then another material down by the legs. It was a hot-ass mess.

Now I look at that picture and I say, *Vivica, that was such a no.* But at the time you couldn't have told me I wasn't cute.

But I got it, though. I was like, *Uh-hmm, that won't happen again.* The criticism can be harsh, but you gotta take it in this business. Sometimes still I'll take a risk, but you better be ready for that feedback and those online comments. Because, baby, the Fashion Police will get you. Hit or Miss, Hot or *Hmm* . . .

I've made mistakes and learned lessons. So the biggest advice I tell all my girls is **"Don't force fashion."** Just because something is trendy does not mean it's for you or your body type. Take me for example: I've got boobs and *ass*ets. I can't wear any trend that's designed for the itty-bitty titty committee, okay? If it ain't got no stretch to it, it ain't working for me.

What you *can* do to keep your look current is to add hints of what's trending. Let's say they're doing too many cutouts, showing off abs and whatever. You can do a cutout down the side of your body that's not so revealing, that's covered with a little bit of lace. Learn to accentuate the positive and not the negative so you don't feel uncomfortable in your outfit—and, perhaps more important, so you don't *look* uncomfortable in your outfit. Confidence is always key.

That goes for everyone. Don't feel because you got a little bit bigger that you have to put on a goddamn muumuu. Whatever size you are, feel good about yourself. It radiates from your whole aura and people see it a mile away. They either say, "Oh, she's not happy," or "Look at her go."

That was important to me as I was making my clothing designs for women, and that's why I offered sizes ranging from 4 to 22. I hate when I see clothes in magazines and you go to get it and it's like, "If you're not sample size, it ain't happening for you." I want to be diplomatic here, but I think that a lot of people in the fashion industry forget that the average, glorious American woman is a size 16. If you forget about those beautiful women, and refuse to make them feel beautiful and included, you're just not good at business and you don't deserve their hard-earned money. My clothes are also not about concealment. No way, honey, celebrate yourself. I did a gorgeous line of lingerie that showcased the glory of women's bodies in sizes 34DDD to 44H for the bras and 6/8 to 22/24 for panties.

I just want to say one more thing to my big guys and girls. Every molecule in your being is loved and special. **You are not beautiful despite your weight; you are beautiful because you're you.** If someone told my sister she was special despite being black, or told my friend he was perfect despite being gay, you and I would throw down for them, right? So why do we accept a beauty standard that makes our curvier girls feel inferior?

My style has evolved as I have embraced this new chapter in my life. When I started becoming famous, I would go for trends. I would *have* to have the perfect Tichina Arnold scarf to match my outfit. I confess I still have to remind myself not to be so matchy and to throw in a pop of color or surprise. Then for a while I was heavily into big jewelry, to my detriment. I was spending way too much money. Then I went into a whole sexy, sexy, sexy thing where it was all about cleavage. That morphed into my rock-and-roll phase, with a tits-and-ass kind of look.

Now I've been trying to do more mature and ladylike looks, thank you, but with a little bit of edge. What I call my "grown woman swag." I will do a little pop of skin, but I had to let go of all my hoochie gear. **Just because I could still fit into certain looks, that didn't mean I still had to wear them.**

When I get red-carpet ready, I always have a theme in mind and I always try to dress to the event. If it's like a music event, you can be a little bit edgier, a little bit sexier. If it's awards seasons like the Emmys or Oscars, you have permission to go all out and be glamorous. I always allow two hours to get ready. I prefer to prep for an event at my house because I have a little salon with a beautiful mirror, lighting, and a chair. It seems like a luxury, but it's actually very affordable and you should consider it if you have space. I turned what would have been a pantry area into my private salon. I have one wall mirrored and framed, and I've got my wigs all lined up in there. Then I got two strips of beauty lights from Home Depot, placing a row of six lights on each side of the main mirror for about thirty dollars a pop. I also put in a comfy chair so that someone can sit and keep me company if they want. I made sure not to forget outlets so I can plug in the hair dryer and curling iron. And that's my little beauty salon. You, too, can have it. Girl, Home Depot can be your best friend.

Here are some other tips to keep you fashion forward:

Invest in one great bag, not ten cheap ones.

I treat myself to one or two good purses per year. Now, I could get three or four pairs of shoes for the price of that $3,000 bag. But it's worth it. My work bag is always an expensive, well-made black bag. I wear black or silver every day when I am working and traveling, so the bag goes with everything. I recently got introduced to the world of Céline. Yes, it's an investment, but that bag will never go out of style. It's a classic, beautifully made and worth the money.

A great bag is also an eye-catcher and conversation starter with other women. This woman in the grocery store the other day was like, "Oh my God, that bag!" Then she looked at me and said, "Oh my God, Vivica Fox!" That bag and I shared top billing, let me tell you.

Your shoes are an advertisement for you.

My romance with shoes began when Patti LaBelle took me under her wing on the set of *Out All Night*, my first series in Hollywood. One time the little wardrobe lady told me my shoes weren't in the shot so they didn't matter. "Oh, just bring any old pair," she said. I wore these flower shoes that I liked.

When I walked in, Miss Patti looked me up and down. "Baaaaaby?" she said, "Please tell me you didn't let them put those shoes on you with that dress?"

"Oh, they're mine," I said. "I think they're cute."

"If you say so," she said. From that point forward, I told myself I would never have anybody give me the side-eye about my shoes. Before my knees started giving me the blues, I used to wear them the higher the better. Now I believe in a good four- to five-inch heel. Most of the collection in my closet are Louboutins—just because I love those red bottoms. But I also favor Jimmy Choo, Giuseppe Zanotti, and René Caovilla. Sometimes those are all the men I really need in my life.

Slay at the office.

Dress appropriately, but always add a little touch of yourself up front. Perhaps a pop of color with your shoe or your shirt. In business meetings, little things can also be talking points—"I love your brooch" or "I like your earrings."

Get a tailor and keep things streamlined.

Get a good tailor. My tailor loves me, but I drive her crazy. I am a bit of a broken record, always making the same requests: "Take in the arms, take off the belt loops, close the pockets, add a zipper in the back . . ." But I say these things to her constantly because I like a fitted look. You hardly ever see me in billowy things because I am a tall girl. And I always tell her to give me a waistline because I work too hard for this waistline. I say a strong "Hell yeah" to shapewear. I don't mean squeezing your guts out wearing the corsets all day, but when you're suited and booted, it's nice to be snatched in, too.

Find a fashion role model.

You can draw strength and inspiration from your own personal fashion icons. I look to mature, sexy women who are around my age. I'm not going to be taking notes from some girl who just broke the pacifier habit, right? So think about people in your age lane who are killing it. For me, the nominees are:

Charlize Theron

First glance: She is tall, beautiful, statuesque. She just makes you go "YAAAASSS, bitch" when she hits the red carpet.

The deeper look: She's never one-note. If she goes really rocker-edgy with the outfit, the material is in a classic black and white. But when she does full prom princess for an awards show, the hair is always very simple.

Jennifer Lopez

First glance: Man, that bitch. She just gets better with time. I love that she's a mature woman who lets you know the best is yet to come.

The deeper look: She dresses totally appropriately for her body and accentuates the positive. She is the queen of using a cutout to draw the eye to what she wants you to see, like her amazing abs. She's about five foot five, and she often elongates her frame by going all leg. And when she does wear a long leg, you better believe she is bare-armed, shoulders out, with her hair styled to death.

Angela Bassett

First glance: This is a woman who took three or four years off to hang out with her kids and live a little bit. And now she's killing the game.

The deeper look: She always has her arms out looking good. You know she does her chair dips and press-ups, so she is going to show you the results in strapless or one-shouldered looks. She'll also mix up classic looks by adding modern touches. A Grecian gown will have little peekaboo cutouts above the waist or a fifties-style cocktail dress will have a new and edgy belt. It's such a smart way to stay current—you know she didn't go to Yale for nothing.

Visit quality, even if you don't take it home.

There are certain stores that are like museums. Care and taste are put into the edit of what they sell. If I am in Manhattan for even a minute for work, I always stop at Bergdorf Goodman. I like to say it's on the corner of Fifth Avenue and opulence. You go in there, and what they have on offer is the best of the best, from the jewelry to the shoes to the bags to the dress and, oh my God, the gowns . . . and, oh my goodness, the coats, the hats . . .

I like them because they've got a good price point. But even if right now you can't afford to buy a jacket that looks like a work of art, you can visit quality, feel it, and then you'll know it when you see it at a price you can afford.

Remember that you're also visiting *people*. A staffer can become your best friend. They can give you a heads-up when a shoe is about to get marked down, and when you really get in good with them, they might let you in on that employee discount. Be kind, learn their names, and be sure to use those names when you greet them.

Okay, you are now ready to get out there and be a fashion warrior. I hope you'll think of me when you're at the checkout with something fabulous, and looking in the mirror at someone *really* fabulous.

DON'T GET OLDER, GET BETTER

Maya Angelou used to say that modesty was a learned habit. I hate when women find reasons to put themselves down when they are really dying to be told they are just fine. Dr. Angelou preferred humility to modesty, so I humbly say that I have great skin. And I can say that because it is part of my job. I have to make sure my complexion is nice and smooth and even, because my face has to be a canvas for a makeup artist to paint. So trust me when I humbly tell you that I know what I'm doing when it comes to looking good no matter your age.

My biggest beauty secret is the cheapest one. It is a little lemon squeeze. Yes, one of those bright yellow plastic lemons you see at your grocery store. You need to drink a ton of water—I try to do 2.5 liters a day—and this will make that water an event. I have one in my bag at all times, and when I rifle through looking for my keys, it's a reminder: "Get your water, girl. Hydrate, hydrate, hydrate." The little guy is under three ounces, so he flies with me right through TSA checks, and he just makes the water special.

As you hydrate from the inside drinking water, you have to hydrate from the outside. As soon as I get up, I spritz my face with Shu Uemura's Depsea Water Rose Mist. I know it sounds exotic and spendy, but it's only about twenty-five dollars and lasts forever. I swear by it. Then I use Kiehl's rosewater toner to clean my face and get it going. I have a steam shower in my home, and I take those showers twice a day. In the morning I put in eucalyptus drops to wake me up, and at night, I put in lavender. It signals my body to get moving or slow down.

As long as we're showering together here, I'll tell you my favorite shampoo and conditioner is the Paul Mitchell Tea Tree Special. If I get to have a day to myself, I'll take time out to condition my hair with hot oil treatments or do a hair mask from Carol's Daughter. One of the things I love about wigs is the versatility and the fact that I don't have to overprocess my hair. I just braid it underneath. (Side note: One of the best parts of having a line of wigs and weaves is customers sending me notes on social media: "I'm wearing Tyce for my date tonight" or "Heading to a job interview with Hayden." *Please* keep them coming, girlfriends.)

I don't wear makeup if I'm not working because I like to give my face a chance to breathe. So I just use lip gloss and the old trick of a little clear mascara on my brows. I am a brow fiend! There's a term that actresses use for a really gifted makeup artist: They can *beat* face. It just means that they do an exquisite job bringing you to the heights of beauty. When I have to have my face beat, I swear by MAC, especially the Studio Fix liquid foundation and pressed powders. When it comes to my eyes, I am a Dior and Chanel girl for my eyeshadow and mascara.

Once a month I do a microdermabrasion and an oxygen facial. I started doing this combined treatment with my esthetician, Sharon Stutz, a little over four years ago, and my God, what a difference it has made in my skin. I think people hear "abrasion," and they are like, "Jeez, what are they gonna put on my face?" They just scrub off those layers of dead skin and keep things smooth. First they clean your face really good. Then they sandblast your skin, and those little aluminum-oxide crystals do their work erasing my lines and wrinkles. Then they do the oxygen, which treats the wear and tear of sun damage and toxins in the air. It also hydrates the skin.

That's an indulgence, but a good investment. One of my Sunday self-care rituals if I am in town is to spend the morning at the Beverly Hot Springs. It's a spa with a natural hot springs right in the middle of Los Angeles. The best part is this gorgeous pool of water, about 103 to 108 degrees. The water has this silky baby oil feel, and it is constantly pumped and drained so it's clean. Then they have this cold, cold, cold water you can plunge into.

They have it done up like you're in a cave, and you just feel transported to another time and place. I take my friends as a treat and make a girls' day of it. One of my best girlfriends, Azja, calls it Lake Minnetonka, after Prince telling Apollonia in *Purple Rain* that she has to purify herself in the waters of Lake Minnetonka. Whenever I run into her, she yells, "*Bitch*, you been dipping in Lake Minnetonka with that good-ass skin of yours."

While I am there, I also get a treatment called Body Care, where they massage you with oil, honey, and milk, wash your hair, and give you a cucumber mask. If it's fifty minutes, and if you're single, it feels like the closest thing to getting some. Who needs a boyfriend? They rub you head to toe, and you get up off that table with the skin of a new little baby.

I put the work in to look good, but when people tell me, "Oh, you're much prettier in person," I'm like, "Well, *damn*, what movie did you see?" They also notice that I'm slimmer than they thought. When I exercise, I don't like to be She-Ra with the weights, since the camera already adds pounds, so I have to keep my muscles long and lean.

That's why stretching has been so important to me. I do it in the morning, no matter where I am, usually right when I get out of bed while my body is still warm from the covers. Should we do one now? How about an upward stretch? I like this one because the first thing you do is straighten your back and hold your head like you're wearing a crown. That's right, my queen or king, wear your crown. Now intertwine your fingers and raise them way high above your head, palms facing the sky. You feel that? Now hold it.

Didn't that feel good? And I am always sure to get in my sit-ups and push-ups, because that's the way to keep your abs and arms looking tight. I also love to hike because I get bored just going to a gym. If I want to go somewhere, I need them to have more than a couple of machines I can do at home. So I will go to a pool for water aerobics five days a week if I am in town, but not just some gym to run in place. You just gotta know yourself and do things you'll stick with. I'm a girl's girl, so if I commit to working out in a class with someone, I'll do it. But when I'm alone, treadmills bring out the to-do lists in my head, so I just end up cutting the run short to get started on work.

Part of staying in shape means staying ready for opportunities. When I got the call that they wanted me for the 2016 sequel to *Independence Day*, I was practically doing backflips. They had been teasing about this sequel on and off for five years, and Will Smith had told me that he wasn't interested in returning.

"Dang, what that mean for me?" I joked to Will. "Sorry to be selfish, what that mean for me? I guess that's the end of my story line, too."

Then I got an email that the director, Roland Emmerich, wanted to see me in person. He wanted to make sure that I was still, let's say, together. Don't act shocked—this is a business and it's twenty years later. They wanted to make sure I still looked good. I get it and let's keep that real. And thank God, I've been taking good care of myself.

We met at his fabulous L.A. house, and when I arrived, his back was to me. I got out of the car and said a sweet "Hi, Roland." He turned around, and I walked up to him with the hips going WHAM! BAM!

"Well, damn, Vivica," he said. "I think you look even better."

Still, I knew I could look even better than his "even better." I couldn't be the stripper in the first one and come back anything but taut for the sequel.

I put my usual plan into action, and I want to share it with you. First off, don't starve yourself. That's deprivation. I need motivation—some fuel in the tank. What I think works is to up your water intake and choose foods that are lower carb, lower sugar, and lower sodium. Here are my other tips:

Start the day keeping it simple.

In the morning I like to have yogurt with blueberries, fresh-squeezed orange juice, and some coffee. And always water. I eat one little pink grapefruit alongside because it's pretty, and because its tartness brings out the sweetness of the blueberries. A mid-morning apple will keep me from making a bad choice for lunch at craft services or in a restaurant.

Cut the portions but amp the flavor.

If you want to have a carb, enjoy half of it and push yourself away from the table. Compensate for that heroic act by banning blandness from your table. I love a lot of garlic and bright flavors in my food. Get out that old lemon squeeze to jazz up grilled fish or chicken. And yes, get dressing, but get it on the side and don't bother with the "low-fat" stuff—it's probably full of sugar and salt to mask its lack of punch. My trick is to dab my fork in the dressing, then stab that salad. When it comes to salad, there is a reason kale and mustard greens are so popular. They just taste better and are more interesting than boring lettuce. What's funny is that my mom used to use kale and mustard greens in her Southern greens to jazz them up. Now she's trendy!

If you don't see it, you won't eat it.

This is true when the waiter comes to ask if you want bread and whether to stock your cupboards full of snacks. If you have a girlfriend at work who is always bringing in unhealthy snacks for people, consider leveling with her and saying, "I love your generosity, but I am really trying here. Will you help me?" If her intentions are sweet, she will listen. If she really is trying to sabotage you, then you've put her on notice. Satan, get thee behind me!

Do you have time to burn calories?

One of the reasons I don't like going to a gym is that it's hard to fit that time in my schedule. Since I don't have time to burn the calories, I have to be stricter about how many I take in. Ask yourself if you would prefer to up your exercise routine rather than count calories.

Keep it moving, Santa.

Listen, I love the holidays. I just hate the food that goes with it. It's simply too much to ask of yourself to spend hours with family, triggering every trigger you've got, I bet, and not eat your feelings. So fill up before a gathering with a healthy snack. I call it taking the edge off. If you can cook—and bless you because I can, but I just don't do it often—make a dish to bring that you know fits your calorie budget.

You need and deserve a cheat day.

Once a week, you've got to reward yourself. Otherwise it's gonna get boring and you'll fall off the wagon. The other day I was in Wisconsin for work. The crew wanted to go to Red Lobster, so I went with them. Of course, I wanted to bond because I liked them, but really it was because it was my cheat day. I had me a cheese biscuit AND a baked potato, I am not gonna lie. My favorite cheat day meal is linguini with clams and a good bread with balsamic vinegar and oil. With wine. And for dessert, a sponge cake à la mode. Or maybe some good old pepperoni-and-sausage-and-mushroom pizza from California Pizza Kitchen. Or perhaps fettuccine Alfredo with chicken, which is really bad. And then more bread . . .

Stop calling it a diet.

Diets are temporary. You're just doing yourself the favor of paying attention to your body and nourishing it. This is not about being skinny or a number on the scale—they don't put your weight on your tombstone. It's about attaining and maintaining strength to last throughout your life.

THE CHANGE OF LIFE IS GONNA COME. SO GET IN FRONT OF IT.

Not long ago, I started going through what people call "the Change" a little bit. Not a little bit—a whole lot! I would be drenched in sweat and have to step away from people to grab my "private summer" fan. That's what my friends call it: a private summer. You look over, and someone is having a private summer in her own little world. "Damn, it's hot!"

You have to get in front of the Change, because it will happen to every woman. The first step is to see your doctor as soon as you suspect it might be happening. (You have a doctor, right? The most important part of paying attention to your body and taking care of it is going to your doctor. I always advise women and men to get their annuals.)

"I think I'm starting to have it," I told my doctor. I didn't even need to say what "it" was.

"No way," he said. "It's too early for you."

I could have just said, "Okay," because at first I was afraid of the Change. Society is not kind to women as they age, and this would put a target on my back. But I persisted, and asked if there was some sort of way to test me to see if I was starting the Change. I wanted to be proactive. He gave me an FSH test, which measures the levels of follicle-stimulating hormones in your body.

He called me. "You were right, Vivica." At first he gave me a synthetic hormone, but that only made me sweat more. With his okay, I decided to handle it naturally.

My first step was to show courage and embrace this new chapter. It was interesting to get to know *me* on the inside, since I'd spent so many years very conscious of how others perceived me from the outside. So I brought that same attention to my body that I brought to prepping for a role.

For me, I found that when I gained ten to fifteen pounds, the added bulk had a lot to do with the severity of the sweats. So I said, *Time to slim down, girl.* And also, when I ate, I listened to what I call "the echo." How did I feel after? What was the echo? I have a girlfriend who charted every hot flash to find the pattern. She found they were tied to three triggers: eating spicy food like Thai or Indian takeout, drinking wine, and dealing with stressful deadlines at work. "I can't do anything about work, and I won't give up my glass of wine," she told me. "See ya later, pad Thai!"

The next step I recommend is to get a little Brookstone fan. How many times have I said aloud, "Where's my fan at?" My little blue guy goes everywhere with me. If you ever want to feel less alone in your hot flashes, check out the reviews for their Breeze Pen. All these corporate girls talking about how it's a godsend for their symptoms. You also need to be okay excusing yourself if you are self-conscious about your hot flashes. Just kind of walk away and do a little pat pat

pat with a small towel in your bag. Some women I know are so in denial about these hot flashes that they don't prepare for them. "Nothing to see here!" Instead, arm yourself with tools that will help you and talk to your sisters about how you're feeling and what steps you're taking to take charge.

My skin started to change, becoming dryer and just feeling thinner. No wonder, since the lowering of estrogen means your body isn't retaining moisture as well. So that's when I made sure I kept up with my facials and started doing more masks at home. I also upped my salmon intake, as I call it, because of those good old omega-3s in fatty fish.

Then your sex drive changes. For me, there was a time that I didn't want anybody touching me, no gosh darn way, so it made me focus on other things. I started getting *another* kind of satisfaction—from work.

And this is what I want to tell you: When you focus on yourself and listen to your body, you'll be surprised how you feel. I was like, *Hmmm. I am being professional, respectful, and considerate. I am going to sleep, I am waking up early, I am looking good,* and *I don't have any drama.*

I was projecting a sense of composure and maturity, and people noticed. I started getting offers of interesting roles playing leader types, and it's because I embraced this new chapter. In interviews, people ask me how I stay so young and I tell them the truth. "I don't. I embrace every new chapter." I am in my fifties now, and many of us aren't interested in passing for thirty-five. Why be an okay thirty when you can be a stunning fifty? That confidence, that presence, is sexy.

I have a theory about why women were once made to feel they needed to go in exile once they started the Change. Some of the most powerful women I have met are on the other side. They are focused and confident and clear about what matters to them. And they're beautiful. Can you imagine a more terrifying thing to insecure men? And what a prize a woman like that would be to a self-assured person.

So repeat after me:

I [say the name of your fine-ass self here] do solemnly swear that at this blessed age of [say your number loud!] I resolve to love my-self, my body, my every curve and wrinkle, and only become more freaking fabulous. So help me, Vivica.

Amen.

PART FIVE

MAINTAINING SUCCESS AS YOU GROW THROUGH CHANGE

YOU WILL WANT TO GIVE IN. DON'T.

If you are now or ever will be in need of a recharge, bookmark this chapter. Because here's something I had to learn: It takes hard work to become successful, but then *being* successful is still hard work. When you're coming up, it can be motivating to hear "No." You say, "Oh yeah? I'll show them." The door slammed in your face just means you kick it harder.

Once you've had success for a while, you might not want to kick as hard anymore. Your poor feet are tired of kicking those doors in. "Buy me new shoes," they say. "Put me up on a couch." You're tempted to lower your expectations.

Don't.

I believe "exit strategy" is a nice of way of saying "quitting." Instead, I believe in evolution strategies. You need them when you've established your career but you're having trouble maintaining momentum. If you're there, here are a few questions I want you to ask before you give up.

How do people perceive you?

I'm not talking about your pretty face. I'm talking about how people view you and your product. Step back and look at yourself as a client or supervisor would. Do you inspire confidence? Meeting deadlines, following up, and maintaining a good attitude are fundamental to reaching your goals, but you have to keep it up. Don't let success make you a failure.

Are you staying current?

If your business is fixing wristwatches and everyone is walking around with an iPhone, you need to reevaluate. This doesn't just apply to people in sales. How are you giving people what they need *now*, not then?

Can you do it yourself?

If you find that you are dependent on someone giving you work or providing your customer base, look at ways you can feed yourself. Can you do what they're doing and reach those people yourself? I have a girlfriend who's a partner in a law firm, and she says she has to bring in business. "Eat what you kill" is the motto in her office. You can't rely on somebody else to keep you fed.

Are you keeping your squad up?

The people you turned to on the way up can still be a resource. Talk to them about your work, and ask them for their honest perspective. They might even be able to partner with you to expand your reach.

Can you channel your skills and passion into a different role?

Think about why you wanted to do the work you're doing. The real essence of it. If you're a chef with a restaurant that is no longer doing well, maybe it's because you like to nourish people and, frankly, you like praise. Can you teach cooking classes? Perhaps there is a food-supply company that needs your enthusiasm and know-how in its sales department. There are alternatives for all careers. A teacher who is tired of dealing with kids can bring that passion to doing corporate trainings. A nurse burned out on the hours and demands can become a legal nurse consultant, helping law firms and insurance companies interpret medical records. That's right, trade that bedpan for the boardroom, honey.

I make jokes, but I know it's hard to face professional disappointment. I have to turn to scripture to give you an important piece of advice. Now, I know Psalm 23 gets a lot of deserved attention. Everyone, from an atheist to a Zen Buddhist, has probably heard this opening line, "The Lord is my shepherd, I shall not want." It's a beautiful testament of faith and hope. But Psalm 34 is the one I turn to when my faith is tested and I feel foolish to have even hoped for something in the first place: **"The Lord is close to the broken-hearted and saves those who are crushed in spirit."**

There was a time in my career where I felt crushed in spirit. I thought it was time to retire—or at least, I thought Hollywood was telling me it was time to retire. So I had to work out my evolution strategy.

I had just entered my forties, and I knew that I needed to start changing up the parts I was going for. I definitely wasn't the young ingénue, and I knew the shelf life on the Hot Chick—at least how it is generally defined—was nearing expiration. You know you can only play those roles for so long and then they start to look for someone else. It's like being on a basketball team. You have your run as the star and, guess what, it's time for your replacement. So I asked myself what I always do when I'm in transition: *What do you have next?*

My first evolution strategy was to try to get a foothold in the mature crowd. So I went up for *The Bucket List*, a Rob Reiner comedy with Jack Nicholson and Morgan Freeman. If you missed the film, it's about two guys who escape from a cancer ward for a road trip to cross off their life's to-dos. I went up for the role of the temptress that Morgan Freeman's character meets in a bar.

I put even more effort than usual into prepping for the audition, because it seemed like my one chance. I nailed it. I'll just say it. I nailed it, and I got callbacks for the role. I felt confident that I was going to work with these amazing men, and I was going to start my career in a new direction.

My agent called and I knew right away it was a pass. "They said you look like Morgan's daughter," she said. "But they really liked you. Rob said he'll always keep you in mind."

So I was still too good-looking to play older roles, but my age meant I was disqualified from playing "the It girl." This happened time and time again. I would pursue something that I thought would get me out of this rut, and I'd have the door closed on me. I felt un-hireable. There were far fewer roles then. Now Hollywood is finally seeing women like us, being hot and being beautiful and being older. How can they deny it when they see Jennifer Lopez, mid-forties, looking gorgeous, and Halle Berry looking amazing in her fifties, and the fabulous Helen Mirren, who's in her seventies and guys still want to jump her bones? Not just that, there are now leading roles for women, ones that demand the presence that experience gives you.

But back then I was out of luck. I refused to get in my own way by saying, "I will only do film." I had already been in the business long enough to know that diversity was the key to longevity. I was not going to wait for Hollywood to throw me a Grandma Suzy role, and I don't want to pull a *Sunset Boulevard* and become a bitter actress. The right part wasn't going to just get handed to me.

So I decided to hand myself the role I wanted by becoming a producer. One of my first projects was coproducing a traveling stage play, *Whatever She Wants*, with Je'Caryous Johnson and Gary

Guidry. Je'Caryous wrote the script for me, calling my character Vivian Wolf. She's incredibly successful but unlucky in love. Ahem. Hell yeah, that totally hit home for me. This was my first time back doing a stage play since I appeared in, deep breath, *Generations of the Dead in the Abyss of Coney Island Madness* in the Mark Taper Forum's 1989 New Works Festival in Los Angeles. That was heavy and dark—though the wonderful director, Lee Kenneth Richardson, went on to direct George C. Wolfe's *A Colored Museum* at the Public Theater in New York. *Whatever She Wants* was more fun, and a lot more work.

I would do the play on the road for four-month stretches, eight shows a week in the starring role, right there in nine of the eleven scenes. Being a producer and star was a lot of work, but I loved the control it gave me—and the channel it gave me for my OCD. I got to worry about *everything*. Because when you're a producer, it's your job to worry about everything! Are you going to run long and have to pay the crew and theater overtime? Is the set right? Are all the price tags off the props? Are people getting *paid*? Which brings up a very important point: Acting and producing equals two checks.

I found that I loved producing, and in that evolution strategy, I found that I was passionate about branding. If my name is on it, Foxy Brown Productions, it has to be quality. People need to understand this. When people give you a title, you have to earn that title. When I have the title of producer or executive producer, people trust me with their money, and they know I am going to finish on or under budget and be on time. Because the more professional you are and the more you show people you appreciate them, the bigger budgets you will get. Your work will lead to another blessing.

Of course, I heard the jokes about me doing the stage plays. People don't take the art of African American plays seriously, and I saw blogs saying "Her career is over!" and "She's on the Chitlin' Circuit!" Hold up. "Chitlin' Circuit" refers to the venues that were safe places for

African American entertainers to perform during Jim Crow. So that's not an insult to me. It says more about the person who uses that as an insult in our present day than it does about black theater. We are blessed to have moved beyond that, and I was just as blessed to find audiences who have wanted to see me in the three stage plays I have produced. When I was feeling down, the African American community was there in those audiences, greeting me with the warm embrace of "There's our girl" every time I hit that stage. It was an opportunity to reintroduce myself to my audience: "I know you knew me as the hot 'It' girl, and now I want you to meet the woman I've become. I hope you like her."

I cherished those experiences, but realized that I still needed a wider audience if I wanted to keep working in film and television. One look at the TV Nielsen ratings told me reality was king. *Survivor, The Bachelor, The Biggest Loser, Big Brother*—there was no reason for networks to do scripted television when they could do these franchises for cheaper. It's called show *business* for a reason. I had to acknowledge that the business was evolving and ask myself how I could fit into this market but still have it be comfortable for me. So when *Dancing with the Stars* called to ask me to be on their third season in the fall of 2006, this time I said yes. I had turned them down twice before, but I did the math. Over twenty-eight million people watched that show. When you are working with someone, you are cobranding, so you have to look at the visibility of that brand. Doing *Dancing with the Stars* would allow me to enter the world of reality but keep my dignity as I showcased my work ethic. Not to mention that I love dancing.

Not enough to love those rehearsals, though. They were grueling. Six hours a day, with three in the morning and three in the evening. My feet went from a size 8½ to a 9! My favorite fellow contestants were Mario Lopez and Emmitt Smith, the former running back. With Mario, he was just so freaking sexy and I wanted to just dive into those dimples. I knew Emmitt would win if I didn't—what a work ethic. Most of my time was spent with my partner Nick Kosovich. I love Nick, but his attitude sometimes needed adjusting. He was cocky, and could be curt with the people working on the show. Including me. But I always deferred to him as a student to a teacher. As we were assigned a dance to perform each week, Nick gave me an amazing tip that helped me as a performer: Approach each dance as a character.

My first was, appropriately, the fox-trot. I fell in the rehearsal, real hard, but I told myself, *You can be tired later.* I went from being kind of under the radar to doing constant press, and I went with it. I did tons of interviews and was lucky to line up events to bring that sudden spotlight to charities I care about, like breast cancer.

We did great, and for four weeks, from the mambo to the Paso Doble, we finished in the top three for the judges' scores. Our tango was even the judges' favorite of the third week. They interview you right after, when you're out of breath and sweaty and just want to lie down. That night the character I embraced was Dorothy Dandridge in *Carmen Jones*, all class and beauty. When I got the three 9s to put me in the lead, I reverted back to Angie Fox winning a basketball game. "Yeah, baby," I yelled. "Yeah!"

So imagine my surprise when I was eliminated the fourth week. On the show, I said, "No tears," but in my head I was thinking, *How the hell did I just work so damn hard, get all those high scores, and get eliminated?* I wasn't the only one who thought that. I went to dinner that week, and this extremely formal French chef came out to see me. We talked about the meal, and then he looked me in the eye.

"By the way," he whispered in his thick French accent, "you were robbed."

I didn't peg him as a *Dancing with the Stars* fan! People's kindness helped, but only so much. I had cleared my schedule thinking that if I worked hard enough, I would at least go further than the fourth week. So, on the spur of the moment, I decided to use this sudden free time to take a vacation alone to Turks and Caicos. *To hell with this*, I said. *I am out of here.*

Now, I never let my losses define who I am. If you sit around harping on your mistakes, there's no room for growth. But I needed a minute, okay?

I was getting ready to head to the airport when my business partner Lita called.

"Vivica, I know you're leaving for Turks and Caicos, but—"

"No."

"My favorite show called and they want to know if you'll come in and audition."

"I'm going—"

"It's *Curb Your Enthusiasm*."

"I don't even know what that is."

"Larry David?"

"Lita, I'm tired," I said. "I am this close to finally taking a break."

She talked me down. She told me how hugely popular HBO's *Curb Your Enthusiasm* was. "I said you're leaving town, and they wondered if you could stop by on the way," she said.

A casting agent saw me on *Dancing with the Stars* and saw how I could be pretty but throw down. They were considering me for Loretta Black, a single mom of two who Larry takes in after Hurricane Katrina. The show was mostly guided improvisation, with Larry and his on-screen wife, Cheryl, choosing what was best, so the audition would also be improv. There were no lines to learn, so what did I have to lose?

"Okay," I said. "But then I'm gone."

"One thing, Vivica," Lita said. "When you go in there, call him L.D."

I went over there with my suitcases in the trunk, ready to just get this over with. Loretta was supposed to be standoffish, so my disappointment with *Dancing* paid off.

Larry wasn't in the room when I got there, and my eyes went to the clock. They told me the improv scene would be about ice cream. I didn't tell anyone I was rushing. I just used my impatience in the scene. When he finally walked in, I was ready.

"Yo, what up, L.D.?" I said. "Tell me something about ice cream."

He burst out laughing. "No one has ever called me that," he said, "I assure you."

And then he said, "That's it."

Then we chatted a bit, but I wasn't sure if "That's it" really meant anything. I zipped up my warm-up suit and left for my flight. When I landed in Turks and Caicos, I was just starting to relax with a piña colada when Lita called.

"Get back on a plane, dear," she said. "You got it."

There went my vacation, but you know I was happy to get on that plane. And what a ride *Curb* was. Right away Larry told me he wanted to strip the "Vivica Fox" away to make the character more raw. "I don't want any Vivica in this character whatsoever," he said. "I want your hair pulled back in a ponytail, and I want no makeup."

"All right, I got you," I said. "I look good without makeup."

He was the glamour cop. I would arrive to set and he'd say, "You have on makeup?"

"Nope. Just a little lip gloss. I swear."

I was only supposed to be on for a little bit, but then they made Loretta a love interest for Larry once he split with Cheryl. They even worked me calling him L.D. into the show. Just like with the "ice cream" improv direction, every morning on the set you would get a little piece of paper with a short outline saying what we were talking about that day. The actors would go in their rooms and start thinking of lines. And you all get together and say your lines and Larry would say, "Okay, that worked and that didn't." The moments that worked, you could massage into a scene. So we would craft and create a whole segment together. You had to be your own writer-producer, but most of all you had to have really thick skin, and then give up final control to Larry. He knew what he wanted, and getting that laugh out of him was everything.

My favorite scene was when I told off his nemesis, Susie Greene. She was this crazy character who was always yelling at him on the show, usually calling him a "four-eyed fuck." She comes to the door screaming at Larry as usual, and my direction was "shut her down."

At first I just yelled that she should watch herself or something, then slammed the door on her.

Larry shook his head. "No, no," he said. "Cuss her ass out."

"I can cuss her out for real?"

"Yeah," he said. "Really go for it."

So I did. That's the take they used, and I knew they had it when I heard Larry's laugh right away. Susie had it coming. People always bring it up when they come up to me about *Curb*. They wrote me off the show, but I was so grateful it lasted as long as it did. I'll say this: It was one of those jobs that you thought would pay a lot. It didn't. But it paid off by opening me up to a new audience who could see me as funny. I used to be able to go to New York and be pretty incognito with no makeup on. Not after *Curb*.

It was a slow burn, though, and I still wasn't getting big movie roles. A lot of celebrities started treating me just a little bit differently when we ran into each other. Yes, Hollywood is a little like high school. There is a cool table, and I could no longer sit there. I call them "sometimey folks." (It's funny, they would barely give me a wave across the room back then, but now they're coming at me to be on their Snapchats or Instagrams . . .)

The movie offers I was seeing didn't excite me so much, but I was getting asked to do things like reality shows and talk shows. The talk-show idea interested me because I liked hosting when I did it as a guest on news and entertainment shows, but at the time it just wasn't quite right. I was offered work hosting reality show reunions, which were becoming more and more popular. I took some of the opportunities, because I wanted to meet the people behind the scenes to figure out what made these shows tick—plus I could also strengthen my hosting muscles. It was hard to miss that the most successful reality shows seemed to be about people getting drunk enough and mad enough to throw drinks at each other. I figured this was a way that I could be a part of these big pop culture moments but let *them* throw the drinks at each other.

One day in 2010 I sat down in my living room and I just said, *Okay, what would I want from a new job?*

The work had to be something I was passionate about, because otherwise it would just be a job. I wanted it to have a touch of glamour to it, because I am a sucker for hair and makeup. If I had to travel for it, all the better, since I get bored hanging out in one place, and I really draw energy from meeting new people. And I needed to have control, because my brand is quality.

I took some downtime, which was weird for me. But it was nice to visit my friends and really spend time with them individually. Not just a hi and a kiss and "I've got to catch my plane." I visited Miami and hung out with my friend James Ansin. He's what I call a connector. He knows a lot of people, and he's just fun to be around. He has a gorgeous penthouse in Miami, and our ritual was to have a light cocktail and then head over to Prime 112 steak house for dinner.

One night we were outside on one of those magical Miami nights at Prime 112, where the air is coming off the water and everyone just looks beautiful. It reminded me of my first days in California. It felt like something new.

"You should get a place here," he said. "You would love it."

"Maybe," I said. "But I need to be in L.A. for work."

He asked what I was working on, and I paused. There were a bunch of things, but the steadiest gig at the time was doing the voice of Angel Dynamite on a *Scooby-Doo* cartoon. I found joy in that, don't get me wrong, because she was actually this really cool character with a lot of backstory for a cartoon. Plus I wasn't in the hair-and-makeup chair for hours. But it wasn't what I wanted to be doing for the rest of my career.

"You know, James," I said, "I'm thinking I have to start planning for something new."

It was the first time I'd said it out loud. It didn't feel like failure. It just felt scary and uncertain.

"What would you do if you weren't acting?"

"I have no idea," I admitted.

"What are you passionate about?"

Every single time someone had asked me that for the last ten years, my answer was always, "My work." But if I didn't have my work, what did I have? Who was I?

"I am passionate about the Indianapolis Colts," I said, joking. "I should call Peyton Manning and see if they need someone. I mean, every morning the first thing I do is turn on ESPN . . ."

James got this little glimmer. "Every morning you watch ESPN."

"And every night, too. I'm a huge sports fan."

"Vivica," he said, "you know who my dad is, right?"

Ed Ansin was the billionaire owner of Miami's WSVN, the local Fox affiliate.

"You'd make an incredible sportscaster," he said, laughing. "I kinda know a guy who might be able to get you a job."

I sat back, and I could see the movie. I'm a sideline reporter, interviewing these accomplished athletes under the lights in stadiums and arenas. We're all so excited to talk to each other—me and Steph

Curry, LeBron James—and then I'm laying down what I know about sports! Or I'm an anchor on a sports show, setting the tone for the show as I get to talk with these great veterans doing analysis. I already had a role model in mind, the incredible Robin Roberts. She started as a sports reporter and anchor for local affiliates, then moved to ESPN before transitioning to being one of the best in the morning news game on *Good Morning America*. This new chapter had what I said I wanted in the next job—passion, glamour, travel, and control—because it would just be me out there, winning or losing on my own.

I high-fived him. I had my evolution strategy, right there over the filet mignon at Prime 112. I had enjoyed hosting and felt comfortable doing live interviews. As an actor, I have already trained myself to really listen to what a person is saying and react. This was the answer to my slump. It felt like I could bolt through a door that was about to slam shut. I would start over, still be on camera, and work my way up again. It would be less money in the beginning, but I have to stress that I didn't see it as a step down. I would still be in people's homes entertaining them, probably making them laugh. And I would get to work with people who cared about what they were doing.

I was so serious about leaving Hollywood that on my next visit to Miami, I had a real estate friend, Tomi Rose, show me a couple of properties in South Beach. The thing was, I was about to line up a local sportscaster salary, so the move had to reflect that.

"Okay," I finally said, "movie star Vivica could live here, but WSVN Vivica . . . ? I need to be real here with you. I have to budget for this future if I do this." We went out of the hot area just a little bit, so I could have more space and privacy, and sure enough, there was this really cute penthouse. I told Tomi I just needed to sleep on it a bit, but I was very close to putting down a down payment.

That week I did an interview with a reporter to promote a gospel fest that I was about to cohost. All the talk of the Lord had me breaking it down for the reporter. I told him I was thinking about making a change and moving to Miami.

"I think Hollywood is a town for . . ." I trailed off. "I've done well being Vivica Fox," I said. "I'm just going to give myself a new challenge."

The interview went right up and I saw those words: "I've done well being Vivica Fox." Dad used to say that when you are ready for that chapter to be over, put a period on it and turn the page. It was the end of my journey as an actress.

And the Lord said, "Wait a minute, we're not done with you yet." I got a call from Byron Allen about a show he was doing with Bill Bellamy, called *Mr. Box Office*. It was a sitcom about a Will Smith– caliber movie star sentenced to community service teaching at a high school in South Central Los Angeles. They had a character who was a "Vivica Fox type."

"Ain't nothing like the real thing, baby," I sang into the phone. There went my Miami plan. A series meant steady work and a schedule I could work around to pursue passion projects. The initial order was for 104 episodes. They wanted to bang them out, filming two shows a week, and that was awesome for me. Plus, I would get to work with wonderful people like Bill, Tim Meadows, and Essence Atkins.

The deal got a lot of press in Hollywood's trade magazines because of the size of the order. And there was my picture on all those articles. There's something about Hollywood where work begets work. People see it's big news that you got hired, and they suddenly want to hire you, too. The calls started coming for more TV work, and I was so grateful.

You see now that I asked myself those five questions I gave you:

How did people perceive me? I wasn't young enough for ingénue roles, but Mama was too damn cute to pull off mature roles.

When I got negative feedback about how I was sustaining my career—like when I did stage plays—I didn't let it get to me. They didn't know the work that goes into building a base of people who will look out for you long-term, and those bloggers certainly didn't pay my bills.

Was I staying current? I saw that roles on scripted television shows were dwindling and reality was only going to grow as networks saw they could get high ratings at low cost. I got on that wave and rode it by hosting reunion shows.

Could I do it myself? Instead of waiting for Hollywood to hand me a role I wanted, I began producing and helped create those roles—and work—for myself.

Was I keeping my squad up? I relied on the African American community to support me and I thanked them by traveling to them. I listened to Lita when she told me not to get in my own way with *Curb Your Enthusiasm*, and I was also honest with friends like James Ansin about my concerns. When I considered a new chapter, I found my inspiration in no less than Robin Roberts.

Could I channel my skills and passion into a different role? I saw sports broadcasting as new way to express my love for entertaining people—and it would be material I loved to talk about. I knew it would be a lifestyle change on the paycheck front, and I was prepared to handle that.

All of this is to say that I've been there. Sometimes life deals you some sucky cards from the bottom of the deck. I'm human, so there's a moment of "Damn, this is awful." But you know, it's all in how you figure out how to play those cards. The deep breath and "Okay, how can we make this better?"

Recently at a lunch party I attended, this girlfriend of mine put her arm around me. "This one here," she said, "she always figures out a new job for herself. Always thinking of something new and wonderful to do. An idea that works and ends up working for you."

"Thank you" was all I could say.

You and me, our dreams are big. There will be moments when our successes grow beyond our dreams, and there will also be times where our success is smaller than our dreams. Either way, hold on to it. Don't give up on your dream, and never, ever give up on you.

IF YOU OWN THE RISK, YOU OWN THE REWARD

n early 2014, my agent, Sheila Legette, gave me a call with another offer. "Listen, the Syfy channel has a movie they want you to do, but they need an answer in thirteen hours."

"Where the hell did they get thirteen hours from?"

"I don't know," she said. "So they want you for *Sharknado 2*—"

I didn't let her finish the sentence. "Yes."

"—as Ian Ziering's—"

"Yes."

"—love interest."

"Yes!"

Why would I want to do a so-bad-it's-good sci-fi sequel about a tornado of hungry sharks? Let me tell you, nobody expected anything of that first film, and I was so happy for Ian and Tara Reid when it became a ratings phenomenon in its re-airings. Perhaps even better, social media embraced the film: 318,000 tweets by 112,000 users. Ian and Tara were in on the joke, and they reaped the rewards for taking a risk on it. So I was so on board.

The plot, such as it was, had me as Ian's high school crush—his chocolate blast from the past—who comes back into his life to see if we can get our swirl on. Didn't happen, but in the meantime there's two sharknadoes coming, and I got to show I could kick butt in action for the first time since *Kill Bill*.

We filmed in New York City, and my L.A. booty was stuck in what had to be the coldest winter ever. At one point we filmed on top of a sixty-five-story building and it was so cold that Ian and I could barely get our dialogue out. We really bonded during the shoot. I had done a guest spot on *Beverly Hills 90210* back when we were babies, but none of our scenes were together. Now we were together all the time, and he was a really fun guy. Every scene was basically us running from airborne sharks, and I had on these tight camo pants and a leather jacket. In one scene we were supposed to fall trying to get away from the sharks, and Ian landed right on my hair. I felt a tug, and I looked down to see two braids on the ground.

"You scalped me," I yelled. "Call TMZ, 'cause Ian Ziering just scalped Vivica Fox!"

While I was filming, the people from *Celebrity Apprentice* called again. They had been after me a few times to do it, but I wasn't sure. By then I had done reality, but in this kind of competition, the camera is on you all the time like a business soap opera. That was a risk, but doing the show appealed to my branding. I was doing more producing and doing well with the Vivica Fox Hair Collection. This would be a good way to introduce myself to America as a business-woman and extend the brand of Vivica Fox. I decided to take the risk and say yes.

The next day, Ian and I were sitting next to each other in our makeup chairs.

"I hear we're going to be working together on jobs back-to-back?"

"On what?" I said.

"I'm doing *Celebrity Apprentice*, too," he said.

I high-fived him. "I will be so sad to see you go home," I joked.

He laughed. Ian is a great guy, and he is even more competitive than me. We talked to Mark McGrath, who was in *Sharknado 2* with us. He had been on *Celebrity Apprentice*, and he pulled no punches.

"They're sixteen-hour days, guys," he told us, "and you'll work every day." He said people get exhausted and testy, which makes for great TV. "It will break you down."

Sharknado 2: The Second One premiered to huge ratings, nearly doubling its tweet count and becoming Syfy's most watched film ever. Important for me, it tripled its numbers in viewers under fifty. I had worked hard to woo that sci-fi audience. I appreciated them. They are loyal, and they will come out to support you. So I put in a lot of time at the San Diego Comic-Con. It was me saying to them, "I know you loved me in *Kill Bill*. Well, guess what, Vivica is still here and she can still kick ass and look good doing it."

I swear I had no idea Donald Trump was a monster. The first time I met him at the start of *Celebrity Apprentice*, he surprised me. He had always seemed like a huckster on TV, but in person he had great presence. He was charming and carried himself with an authoritative tone. Whether it was a complete fabrication or not, the feeling was that you couldn't come on this show and bullshit him.

He transmitted that bottomless pride to everyone around him. You were doing a reality show competition, but he made you think you were curing cancer. We all called him Mr. Trump, and you found yourself truly wanting to please him. I can see why he inspires such loyalty from people in his inner circle. I certainly fell for it.

I will say that it was the most racially charged set I have ever been on. Ever. There were three other black contestants, Keisha Knight Pulliam, Terrell Owens, and Kenya Moore. The Trump family carried themselves in a certain kind of way around the contestants. "We're here. You're there. Yes, we're Daddy's spoiled little kids." I chalked it up to living a privileged life. We were the help.

Ivanka is the one who inherited her father's presence. When she walked into a room, she acted like royalty and you treated her as such. I think because she really thought her father was some kind of king. Whatever the reason for it, I commend her for that commanding presence. She's definitely the savviest of the lot.

Don Jr. acted the part of a gentleman, and so clearly emulated his dad. Eric was another story. He was such a cold fish, but as we did the show, I realized that he was really just painfully shy. It must have been so difficult growing up with all of these personalities.

The one who seemed to have it worst was Melania. She seemed cold when I first met her and never warmed up. She was stiff, like it hurt her to move. At the time, I thought she was just playing the role of the kept wife to the hilt. Knowing what we know now, I think she was just really lonely.

Having lived on Planet Trump for my stint on *Celebrity Apprentice*, I can see why they have such an inflated view of themselves. Their name is inescapable. You woke up and his name was on the TV and on the bath products. You drank Trump Ice water and sipped Trump wine. I'm surprised I didn't turn into a damn Trump. The thought of Vivica A. Trump makes my blood run cold!

When we got there, Ian had prepared so much. Lord, he had watched every episode and had all but taken himself to Trump University. I was impressed, and I have to say that it was always nice to see his handsome face smiling at me on the tough days of the show. He would ask me if I was hanging in there when a lot of other people just wanted me to fall. As actors, we also had an advantage, I think, because we know how to take constructive criticism and then sharpen our game.

Mark was right, it was tough. I would say it was even tougher than *Dancing with the Stars*, because that you could walk away from. We were getting up at four in the morning and working until midnight, constantly hurtling toward one deadline after another. There were also some reality TV veterans there, and they had that drama muscle amped and ready to create "scenes" that would get airtime. Like clockwork, the worker bees among us who took the challenges seriously would become exasperated and find ourselves inadvertently playing right into their scenes. What was a very superficial bit of role-playing to them was to me very real. At night, finally alone, I would lay out my clothes for the next day, because there was always such a rush in the mornings. In bed I would lie awake and my mind wouldn't shut off. I would fixate on what I could have done to make the interaction more positive, or what I really wanted to say to someone.

I constantly fantasized about leaving and just saying, "Okay, I'm good, see ya." I shared this with Lita, who knew just what to say.

"So you want to quit," she said.

"I didn't say 'quit,' I just want off the show."

"So, quitting," she said. " 'Vivica Fox Quits *Celebrity Apprentice*' is the headline. You're quitting."

That was the push I needed. I never want to be seen as a quitter. I had to remember that this was not a show about business—it's a show about people with strong personalities forced to live under extreme pressure. That's why people crack.

So I guess I have to talk about Kenya.

Okay, from the start I knew she was trouble. Everybody did. She cast herself as the villain. It hurt me because I had known Kenya for years and always thought, *Wow, such a pretty girl*. I root for my girls, and I want them to be Miss America or Miss USA or whatever the hell title she won because she will definitely correct you in that nasal voice of hers: "No, it's Miss . . ." Baby, you won a title, shut up. But much respect to that because she did win. BITCH.

So I was sad to see the transformation in her. Becoming a "star" on *Real Housewives of Atlanta* had changed her into this reality chick who would stab you in the back for fame. Or spare change.

That behavior was why I was so sure she was the culprit when my Samsung Galaxy phone went missing in our dressing room during the King's Hawaiian challenge. (I can't see those buns without shaking my head.) This isn't an ad for Samsung, by the way. I paid $600 to have it replaced and get a new one by noon. When I finally had a phone again, I was so busy working that I didn't check my Twitter. Big mistake.

As project manager of the challenge, Kenya failed miserably. So in the boardroom she went after me. It was no secret she hated me. "If Vivica tries to throw me under the bus in the boardroom for no reason, I will not only throw her under the bus," she said on the show, "I will pick up the bus and drop it on her several times. Then I will get in the bus and drive over her. Then back up and drive over her again."

Well, she threw herself under that bus by doing a bad job, but she still tried to make good on her promise to destroy me. In the boardroom, when it was clear she was the most likely to leave, she pulled a Hail Mary—or more likely Hail Satan—and accused me of being erratic.

"Vivica has had wild ups and downs, emotionally she has been very angry at times," she said. "I've seen her go from these hot flashes to being all over. I saw a tweet from her the other day saying that she was going through menopause."

She tried to justify trying to use my age against me by saying I had tweeted about it—while my phone was missing.

That started this hunt to find the tweet, which I present in all of its typo glory and grammatical nonsense:

"This menopause id killing me I can't think straight. im acting a damn fool half the time 50 just isn't sexy"

Donald Jr. read it aloud, and he agreed that it seemed odd that all my other tweets were things like "Have a blessed day." Plus it was the only random tweet in the time my phone was missing. Now, I will be sexy until the day I die. On my worst day, I am a sexy girl. I never would have tweeted that, not just for my vanity, but because it would have dragged down my girls in their fifties. Also, I know how to write a sentence, okay?

What a coincidence that Kenya brought up that I tweeted about menopause to back up her claim that I was erratic. Even Mr. Trump said to Kenya, "Why are you so nasty to everyone?"

Kenya was so unbelievably fortunate that she was dealing with Vivica Fox. Because Angie Fox from Indy would kick her ass on 38th and Emerson. To avoid calling her a toxic bitch on NBC, I coined a term that went viral: "toxic trick." Honey, people loved that.

Kenya continued to deny she took my phone, but the boardroom showdown was all anyone could talk about on the entertainment shows, and it made for good watercooler talk. Nice try, trick. She was good for business. I had to laugh a little while later, when Kenya somehow got herself into a Golden Globes after-party. She sidled up to Lupita Nyong'o and asked for a picture with her. Apparently she got denied because Kenya tweeted: "@Lupita_Nyongo refused 2 take pics After 2 movies #girlbye"

A reporter asked Lupita, who you know I love, about the "incident."

"Who is Kenya Moore?" Lupita said. **Exactly.** #girlbye.

I finished in the top three out of sixteen contestants of *Celebrity Apprentice*, and I won $70,000 for my charity, Best Buddies. So I consider myself a winner. I left with my head held high. In my last boardroom meeting, Trump asked me if I thought Leeza Gibbons deserved to go home before me. I was honest and said Leeza was a better choice to stay. People were really surprised by that, considering it is such a cutthroat game. But Leeza had consistently done a wonderful job, earning more cash in the competitions. I knew the next challenge would be a fund-raiser, and I knew she would shine at that. She won the season, and I was genuinely proud of her. Game recognizes game, and more than that, good women support good women.

One more thing about Mr. Trump: I don't dislike him because he's a Republican. I don't dislike anyone simply because of a label or lifestyle. I believe in uniting people, and he's done a terrible disservice to this wonderful country by trying so hard to divide us. He planted a lot of ugly seeds, seeds that will take us awhile to get past. But we will. We have no choice. I believe that united we stand, divided we fall.

When *Celebrity Apprentice* was over, I thought that that was just five and a half weeks of my life that I'll never get back. But when it finally aired, it led to something a lot better.

The night that epic boardroom showdown with Kenya aired, my phone was ringing nonstop. I was just about to put it away and give myself a break when I got a call from Lee Daniels. I have known him for many years, but never had the chance to work with him. Before *Precious* came out, we watched it together on his laptop in a hotel room in Miami. I knew it was a masterpiece. I remember grabbing his arm and saying, "Thank you." He had a vision that put a spotlight on the lives of black women whose stories have not been valued enough to show on-screen. I then watched his continued rise, getting such fantastic performances out of Oprah in *The Butler* and Taraji in *Empire*.

Lee didn't even say "Hello" and just got right into it. "Bitch!" he said. "Bitch! Gawd, Vivica, that boardroom scene!"

He was talking a mile a minute, which is how his brain works.

"Lee, she tried me," I said.

"You had that Diahann Carroll *Dynasty* thing going on. Michelle Obama brought to the limit."

"She is lucky I'm a classy lady, right?"

"Baby, I'm going to figure out some kind of way to get you on *Empire*."

"Um, hello, stop reading my mind."

"Okay, let me think," he said. "But I want you to be a part of my family."

Now, in Hollywood when you hear that "Oh, I would love to work with you!" thing, you don't think much of it. But Lee has always kept his word.

He called me a few months later. "Would you mind playing Cookie's older sister?" he asked.

"I'd play Cookie's grandmother, honey."

"I don't want you to be coming in here like Cookie," he says. "I want you to be different."

The contrast he created is that my character, Candace, is a bougie, rich suburbanite who left the tough streets of Philadelphia in the rearview of her Mercedes and never looked back. She's got a white husband, two kids, and when an issue with their sister Carol pops up, Candace has to step into Cookie's world. They're both rich, powerful women, but how they present themselves to the world is completely different.

Lee knows what a ferocious, amazing actress Taraji is, so he told me he needed someone who, every now and again, could just show the slightest hint of toughness underneath Candace's Hermès scarf.

Did I mention her clothes are gorgeous? Candace goes into her Park Avenue lunches in the armor of her fashion. Her dresses rarely even have patterns, because she never, ever wants to clash with her surroundings. She's a bit of a chameleon that way. And I love that she is a mature woman who still presents her shape, but tastefully. As the sisters have spent time together, they've sort of rubbed off on each other. Cookie listens to Candace in a way she doesn't to others, and Candace is dropping a lot of that bougie act as she gets more comfortable straddling between her world and Cookie's.

I was excited because me, Taraji, and Terrence go back like Kool-Aid. Terrence and I did *The Salon* together in Baltimore, back when I was a teary mess. The first time Taraji and I were in our makeup chairs together for *Empire*, we had a real sister moment. She leaned over to me. "This is so crazy," she said. "I'm so glad that you are playing my sister."

We shoot in Chicago, so when it's cold, what the hell else is there to do but hang out and talk? Gabourey Sidibe and I sing old-school R&B together, like Keith Sweat's "Nobody," and maybe over a little vodka, we old-timers talk the young ones through the trials and tribulations of fame. We keep it positive, though. "Welcome to the ride."

I host *Empire* viewing parties because it is so satisfying to see people react to my scenes with Taraji. I hosted one in Hollywood, and there were all sorts of oohs and aahs and laughs, because those sisters really know how to get under each other's skin. This young black woman came to me for a photo, and I hugged her tight as the flash went off.

She got all serious. "Thank you," she said.

"Oh, baby," I said. "*Thank you* for coming out to support *Empire*."

"No," she said. "Thank you. I can't remember seeing two black women together on TV looking so fabulous and being so smart. Thank you."

It was like that moment when I thanked Lee for *Precious*. It's the return on my investment of time in *Celebrity Apprentice*, and of Lee's investment in me.

If I wasn't already feeling like this was my comeback moment, I got to tell the world that I would be back in *Independence Day: Resurgence*. It felt like *my* resurgence, to be honest. Me and those aliens were back, baby. There had been talk about a sequel for five years. And I had resisted every urge to call producers and say, "What about me? What about me?" I was afraid the answer would be, "Bitch, what about you?" I told myself to just be patient.

But here I was. We started shooting in Albuquerque, New Mexico, in the beginning of May 2015. Stepping on that set again was like walking into a high school reunion. Sometimes you go back and you're like, "Oh, Lord, keep it moving!" Not this time. I got to see all my old friends again, like Jeff Goldblum, Judd Hirsch, and Bill Pullman. It was also fun to have scenes with the icons in the making, the whippersnappers like Jessie T. Usher and Liam Hemsworth.

In the beginning, I was surprised that they were a little starstruck, even Liam to some extent. So I remembered what Tom Cruise did for me on *Born on the Fourth of July*. I went right up to each one and said, "Hi, I'm Vivica." It broke the ice.

My character, Jasmine, had retired from the pole, I am happy to report. She went on to become a hospital administrator, and has mentored her son to follow in Will's footsteps, and to not be afraid of success. It's kind of what I want to tell you. You're about to start your own journey. Don't be afraid.

My first day on set, I did my wardrobe fitting, and then I was off for the evening. We all hung out a little bit, but then I went back to where I was staying a little before eight. I poured a glass of Pinot Noir and sat out on the patio by myself. I watched the sun set, gorgeous reds and yellows painted across the sky. I knew I had to pray.

"Thank you, God," I said. "You brought it back. You brought it back."

I remember saying it twice, because I was still in such disbelief. He rewarded my patience, and the risks that I took. I sipped the wine, and watched those reds darken to the colors of a phoenix in the sky.

Do not count me out, and do not ever count yourself out. We will rise, we will rise.

YOU PAY THE COST TO BE THE BOSS

When Oprah asks you to do something, you say yes. I got a call in 2014 that she was doing a new series for OWN. The premise was that she would invite some of her favorite guests to come back and talk about lessons learned since they appeared on *The Oprah Winfrey Show*. I was touched and honored when she asked me to come on.

I met her for the first time back when I was thirty-two. She had a bunch of us actresses on the show to talk about beauty secrets and the lengths people go to look good. I cracked her up because I admitted that one of my tricks was shaving the hair on my arms and my hands. I still do, not because I have a lot, but because I like the way it keeps my arms looking toned in photographs. We clicked because I think we shared a realness. You don't expect an actress to say she shaves her knuckles and her toes.

This time we met one-on-one, no audience, on a set in Los Angeles. When I arrived, I saw they had a huge array of photos of me from films and magazines, a sort of scrapbook of my life. I was looking at them when Oprah walked in wearing this gorgeous pink blouse, and it's exactly what you think: You hear a choir of angels in your head saying, "Opppprraaaahhhh!" We shared a hug—she gives the best hugs—and she said, "Okay," which signaled everyone that we were about to get right into it.

What I love about her, besides everything, is that she has a wonderful way of just making you feel comfortable. She has an art to getting you to open up. When you do interviews, now more than ever people are looking for the headline: the "She said what?" moment out of an hour of conversation that will get retweets and clickthroughs. Trust, Oprah doesn't need anyone for publicity.

She teased me right away as the cameras rolled, remembering that when I was first on her show, I admitted I was terrified that I was about to be thirty-three. Now here I was with age fifty in the rearview. We laughed, and she looked away from me for just one second, saying she knew I have a great relationship with my godchildren. And then she turned the high beams of her gorgeous brown eyes on me.

"Do you ever miss being a mother?"

"Of course," I blurted out. I surprised myself. I didn't know how close to the surface that feeling was.

"Really?" she said. "I didn't expect that answer."

"That's the biggest regret of my life," I said, "that I didn't have a child."

As she nodded, I just started to speak the truth that I had frankly made myself too busy to fully face. I talked about running into my friend Halle Berry on the red carpet. We did *Why Do Fools Fall in Love* together, and I just had to tell her how beautiful I think her daughter, Nahla, is. "Vivica," Halle said, "if I knew then what I know now, I would have had five of them."

I hadn't thought about that conversation in a long time, but there it was. Halle's regret was that she didn't start sooner. Mine was that I had completely missed my chance.

"I don't get to see my eyes in a child," I told Oprah, "and I think that's something that I'll miss."

I spent my career hustling and moving forward. If I don't have time to think, I don't have time for regrets. My father's old adage, "Keep it moving." But you can't lie to Oprah. She gets to the heart of you.

Oprah and I went on to talk about being aunties. "We give the best gifts, don't we?" she said. Oprah is always honest, too, and she is frank that she never dreamed of being a mother. The year before our interview, I remember she got real with *The Hollywood Reporter*. "If I had kids, my kids would hate me," she said. "They would have ended up on the equivalent of the *Oprah* show talking about me; because something would have had to suffer and it would've probably been them."

Something would have had to suffer. Bless her for honesty. Because I want you to know that there are sacrifices to success. We've talked about drive and harnessing your inner power, but now we have to talk about the very real consequences of focusing on a dream. To do what I love and what God has called me to do, I need to be able to jump on a plane at a moment's notice. Opportunities are there to be seized, and I have to be ready.

Where the regret comes in is when I realize that no one told me the truth: **Yes, you can have it all, but only in stages.** I spent a long time beating myself up that I couldn't balance a career in Hollywood with the relationship I would need to raise a family. I thought I had to do it all at once. But I'm here to tell you that you don't get it all.

Now, grab a Kleenex and dry your tears, because you're not alone. Nobody has it all, whether you're married to the love of your life or married to the job of a lifetime, so stop beating yourself up about it.

Accentuate the positives in your life. Squeeze those lemons into lemonade.

Let me tell you, my godson Christian is a little glass of sweet lemonade with extra sugar. He is six now, but he was my first godbaby, setting the stage for my other beautiful godchildren, Quinny, Lola, Eugene, Love, and the newest addition, Iman. They call me G.G., which is short for Gorgeous Godmother, thank you. Christian only recently learned about "Vivica Fox," because he is used to seeing me incognito during my time with him, wearing no makeup and a baseball cap. But recently I went to Christian's peewee softball practice, and I was all dressed up because I came rushing from a photo shoot to make practice on time. I had promised him I'd be there, and through hell and high traffic, I was gonna be there. So when he saw G.G.'s car and out walked Vivica Fox, he did this double take.

"I'm just wearing my Vivica Fox uniform," I said.

"But you're still my G.G., right?"

"Always, honey."

Throughout the game I was cheering all the kids on, and because it was a sports event, I found myself slipping into my full Indiana voice. People were looking at me, throwing in a "That's right, Vivica!" here and there, and it was cracking me up. Afterward, I took him and his wonderful mom, Jazsmin, to sushi. Folks kept smiling at me or politely said hi. So as he ate his little chicken meatballs, he asked me how all these people were my friends.

"Oh, I just love everybody," I said. "When you smile, Christian, people smile back."

Jazsmin called me that night after she put him to bed. She told me that as he was in his pajamas and about to brush his teeth, he asked her a question.

"Mommy, who does G.G. take care of?"

"What do you mean?" Jazsmin asked.

"Does G.G. have any kids?"

"Well, no."

"Then who does G.G. take care of?" he asked.

"Well, she loves taking care of you," she said, "and her family."

"But doesn't G.G. need somebody to come from her?"

As Jazsmin shared this, I was quiet on the other end of the line, caught between feeling a little sad for myself and so proud that this little wonder of a boy was concerned about me.

The next time I saw Christian, I was in my G.G. baseball cap and jeans. I told him that I heard he was worried I didn't have any kids. "I'm very, very happy," I told him. "Don't worry about me."

"Okay," he said. "I just want to make sure you had someone."

"You're my someone," I said, meaning every word and hugging him so he wouldn't see me welling up. Kids just want to be sure of things, and he wanted to be sure that I had love. And I do.

Being an auntie is underrated. Listen, take it from Oprah and me. At my age, I am getting the best of both worlds. The kids can't wait to share things with me. "I know all the colors of the rainbow, G.G.!" Or "Look what I can do!" as one them does a topsy-turvy somersault. They've helped me rediscover having fun. As an auntie, I get to see them facing the small, friendly challenges of childhood and marvel as they overcome them. Like the other day I took Christian to the mall and I announced in my infinite wisdom that it was time for big-boy shoes.

"Okay, Christian," I said, picking up a pair of red sneakers. "You're gonna learn how to tie your shoes."

Jazsmin whispered to me, "He doesn't, uh, he doesn't know how to tie his shoes."

"Sure he does," I said. "He's five. He's gonna know how to tie his shoes."

Jazsmin started talking to him about bunny ears, and I rushed in like I was the director of the scene. "Bunny ears?" I said. "Here, Christian, put it in the loop, wrap it around, and put it through the hole."

"He doesn't have that coordination yet," Jazsmin said. Then she started laughing. "Vivica, you have forgotten what it is to be five. You have to learn with the bunny ears."

So instead of me giving him a hard time, I said, "Just do the bunny ears and you'll advance."

"Okay," he breathed out, "but can I get the shoes?"

"Damn— Darn right, you can," I said.

You will miss a lot building your empire—there's no getting around it. If that empire is your family, then be proud of it. If your empire is built outside the home, when you have a measure of success, you will be able to set aside more time for your loved ones. Now I want to be at their graduations, their weddings, their everythings. These things are important for me to be at, especially now that I can make space in my life for them.

I paid the cost, and now it feels like an indulgence to be quiet and still in my beautiful house in the morning. I love taking my cup of coffee and lighting my candles and looking out at my backyard and seeing my roses bloom. It's the simple, little things. It's not about having to have a big car or diamonds, though I do have my guilty pleasures. Now, it's not a requirement to be "done" all the time. I'm not that kind of babe. I am enough for myself.

Which leads me to this next very important lesson about being in the winner's circle: **Don't miss the opportunity to say no.**

The other day somebody offered me a project and I was *so* happy to say no. The last few years I have been such a worker bee, focusing on rebuilding my career. I didn't feel I had the luxury to turn down anything. The instinct is to say yes, and then figure it out schedule-wise. It is a gift to be able to say, "I'm not available, best of luck with your project." Don't be a bitch about it, because they could be on the receiving end of your résumé when their next project is your dream project. But, yes, relish when the hustle you've put into being a boss means your schedule is filled with jobs that you love doing.

People will try to make you say yes out of obligation. My assistant Darren has a line: "Oh, honey, they're bad for business. They shouldn't even be associated with the brand of Vivica A. Fox. Bad." It's not being stuck-up. It's knowing your worth.

I honestly just discovered my worth in my fifties. It started when I began to judge my value by how I felt about me. I used to ask myself, *What deal did I just make? What in crowd am I in?*

Now, I'm a grown-ass woman. I paid the cost to be my own boss, so I get to choose the value of my crowd. And it feels good.

IT'S FUN TO BE THE HEAD CHICK IN CHARGE

July Fourth weekend of 2014, I accepted my work buddy Ian Ziering's invitation to watch him cohost at Chippendales in Las Vegas. Twist my arm, right?

It was a gorgeous show at the Rio All-Suite Hotel and Casino. The place was packed, and I looked around at all these women just having fun and screaming. Ian was amazing, and it was a quality production. But as I was watching the show, I had one question: Where were the brothers at?

Whoomp, there he was, off there in the corner. I had to squint a little to see his fine self. He was so gorgeous, and when he had a little moment, the place went wild. I turned to my friend and smiled.

"The darker the berry," I said.

"The sweeter the juice," she responded. And the women all around me seemed to agree.

It sort of reminded me of when I sat in the theater with my girlfriends watching *Magic Mike*. Now, I loved that film and I think

Channing Tatum can get it, but I kept waiting for the black guy. And he never really showed up, did he? My producer mind started going, thinking that whoever did a *Magic Mike* with beautiful men of color and a great story would have a gold mine presenting something for everyone.

So when I was invited to be in the movie *Chocolate City*, I said, "Yes, please." It wasn't just a black *Magic Mike*. There was a real story about a fine-looking man financing his college tuition by shaking what his mama gave him. Yours truly played his mama. I got to meet some of these dancers, and a lot of them had all sorts of reasons for stripping. Some had families to provide for, and some just plain loved the attention and fun. Their stories were fascinating to me.

I wanted to tell those stories, and also provide a lot of eye candy. That was the start of *Vivica's Black Magic*. I came up with an idea to do a reality show where I audition hundreds of men to find eight male exotic dancers to take on the journey of getting a residency in Las Vegas. Once the eight were chosen, there wouldn't be eliminations or silly challenges—this wasn't about becoming Stripper of the Year, okay? It was about starting a business. I would put my own money in and put my name on it—gotta have skin in the skin game, right? High stakes and tight abs just made sense as good television—or more, as the possibilities seemed endless: a tour, residencies elsewhere . . . the gift that keeps on giving.

It had to be done right, though, because my brand is quality. I didn't want a drunken fighting show, and I wanted this to have me as a businesswoman at its heart. So I pitched it to Howard Owens at Propagate Content. He co–executive produced *Biggest Loser* and *MasterChef*, so I knew he understood the power of combining storytelling with a challenge—and I was ready to throw in some heat. I marched into his Hollywood Boulevard office in the sleek business outfit that showed the image I wanted to present on the show: what I call "Head Chick in Charge."

He loved the idea, and told me there was a gentleman from Lifetime in the office today. The channel had had a lot of success with *Surviving Compton* and the Toni Braxton biopic, so they were looking for edgier programming. "Are you ready to pitch it now?"

I seized that opportunity right quick. This show was a gift to women, and what better place than Lifetime? So we did the surprise pitch, and my passion for the project sold it. Let me tell you, pitch to greenlight in an hour is unheard of in Hollywood. **When an idea fills an obvious need and you pitch it right, you can get what you want.**

We held auditions and narrowed it down with callbacks. When we found our eight men, I called them my elite eight. They were already stars in different parts of the country: Atlanta, L.A., D.C., New York . . . It was an opportunity to show all the different hues of black men, from light to dark chocolate. We even had a white guy, Greg Jackson, who calls himself White Chocolate. He's a former stockbroker! Each man had an it factor, but they were a little rough around the edges. One would be an amazing stripper, but just an okay dancer. There'd be a good dancer who had to learn how to sell the fantasy of sex. Maybe in some of these clubs they were in, it was enough to put your whatever in a woman's face, but this had to be quality. I had to teach them that a woman who comes to a *Vivica's Black Magic* show deserves to be seduced. She is an empress, and you are earning her attention. The thing that gets me every time is an *Officer and a Gentleman* look. I love to watch a man getting out of his crisp uniform.

I would say that all of the men needed to learn how to take constructive criticism. Honey, the show was a crash course in the male ego. Watching the final product was fun, but wow, these eight alpha men could get in their feelings!

"Why aren't I up front?"

"Do I need to lose weight?"

"Vivica, the other guys ain't being nice to me . . ."

And of course, being the Mama Bear I am, I gotta go off on everybody. Then I would get the whole story. I'd hear, "Pull back, Vivica, what really happened is . . ." I would go back to this bashful hunk and get the full truth. "Why you lying to me? Anyway, here's a drink and shut up. And do an ab roll."

Yes, I was very hands-on, but I kept my hands off the men. What's funny is that as I did the press rounds for the show, a big question was always if it was hard to resist hooking up with these guys. The people asking me sometimes just assumed I hooked up with my employees. Um, no way. Mostly the guys thought of me as Mama Bear, anyway, but a couple of times they would say, "Vivica, you fine as hell."

"And I'm still your boss," I would say. "And I don't shit where I eat. So back that thing up and keep all of them little eyes and that flirtations that work on them other girls. That ain't workin' on the boss lady."

I really was the boss. When I walked into that room with my "Hola! Hola! Hola!" these eight strong-willed men snapped to attention. I put $300,000 of my own money into this, and I was looking for investors. So I had to make sure I taught these boys to not be selfish and not waste this opportunity. It had to be a Las Vegas–ready production. I was also going into my own pocket to make sure my girls in the audience had some money for tipping. Hell or high water, I was gonna give them the ultimate girls' night out. I always referred to the audiences as my guests. If I realized maybe there was a bachelorette party or a birthday girl in the house, I would gift them something from my Vivica Fox clothing line. It wasn't for the show or cross-promotion. I just wanted to leave the people saying "Wow."

Some people working behind the camera didn't get that. "Hmmph, black stripper show." I would come into the venue on some nights, and the location would be dirty, or it wouldn't be decorated.

"Are you going to have drinks or appetizers for my guests?" I would say. "You're asking them to come at six-thirty?"

"Oh, but we don't want eating on camera."

"But you want my people to sit around with nothing?"

This is the quality I am talking about. I wanted light foods, finger foods. Put up some chicken wings in this bitch. Open up the bar for wine and beer. Girls aren't big heavy drinkers. A small investment of money and effort would get a huge result.

The night turned out amazing. "See, this is how show night is supposed to be," I said. But reality shows, they want stress. They got some stress, but it wasn't the fun kind they wanted. They were like, "Oooh, stop pissing her off."

Because for me, when you have unnecessary stress, it trickles down. If you're the leader and you're walking around like a stress case, guess what, your production is going to be a stress case. When everybody is happy and people feel respected, they will bend over backwards and give you the world.

GO FAR, BUT DON'T FORGET WHERE YOU CAME FROM

This Head Chick in Charge is writing to you on the plane back from Indianapolis. We Fox kids just wanted to spend some time with Mom. Part of this next chapter in my life has been realizing that my mother is becoming more fragile and my time with her all the more precious.

Whenever I walk in that house, the creak of that screen door sends me back in time. I hug Mom, and I'm little Cartwheel Angie again, bursting with energy. The house is immaculate, but it has remained unchanged since I was a little girl. When I sit in the front room where I used to dance, it is easy to look at the dozens of family photos in Mom's little gold frames and think about all the dreams I had right in this space.

My siblings all came to the house. When we're together, it's interesting how we still play the same roles in our family after all these years. Perhaps the same is true of yours. You play to your strengths or you stick to your habits. In my own family, again and again I see my handsome big brothers, Marvin and Sandy, and my sweet beautiful sister, Sug, playing the same roles. Marvin is still our "Sarge," ready to take on any heavy lifting for us girls and bring it home with military precision. Sandy is our Sandy, mellow about all things except his fierce love for our mother. I'm the worker bee. If we need something, I can provide. "Okay, now how much is that going to be?" It is my privilege to pay for things, and it's why I work. There are so many day-to-day things that I cannot be there for, and I embrace moments when I can be a provider for my exceptional, loving family.

And of course Sug has remained that Mama Bear, seeing to the health of our parents. She is so strong for others, and one of my roles is to tell her to be strong for herself and for the beautiful family she has created on her own. She is a jewel for our family.

This weekend I told her how I have been reflecting on what she has done for me all these years.

"It must've been hard for you to be so responsible as a kid," I said.

She sighed. "Yes, it was," she said. "I had an old soul at my young age."

"Sug, you know I adore you," I said. "Thank you for all you've done for me."

"But we had fun, too," she said. "Do you remember when we went sledding at Dad's?"

How could I forget, since I near about broke my neck? Dad was living in Cleveland for a bit, and he took us sledding when we visited him in December. I was doing fine, but then some neighbor girl jumped on my sled. She made the sled go even faster, so when we hit the slope, we were airborne.

"The sled went one way, and you and that girl went the other!" Sug said, laughing hysterically.

I was laughing, too, remembering Sug's face when she ran over to make sure I was okay. Angie couldn't get hurt on her watch.

We could have reminisced all day, but there was work to do. Mom was finally letting us update her bathroom for her, but only if we did it ourselves. "I don't want a bunch of strangers in here," she said. Thank God Marvin and me are handy.

My brothers, Sug, and I all drove over to Walmart, and it was just cool to be out with them. I loved flying under the radar in my baseball cap, because to me they're the stars. I tend to grab their arms for a squeeze while we're walking, because I get so excited when we're all together. It's different from when they visit my world. This is our home.

They know I love shopping and interior decorating, so there was a lot of teasing. "Okay, Angie, come here and pick the towels." And, "Ask the expert about this toothbrush holder." My big line was "We need a pop of color," so they started saying that constantly through the store. "What's the pop of color?" For the record, my mother's pop of color was green.

Nobody recognized me until we had to go back for an exchange. Let me tell you, then I was Vivica Fox. "Okay, we didn't need these in silver, honey, but we need some more of that stick-on tile that looks so fabulous. Oh, thank you so much, sweetheart."

Marvin and I did the work, listening to some fine music on my phone. I sang along to "She's a Bad Mama Jama"—my song if there ever was one. Sug worked in the kitchen cooking with Mom, and every now and again good old Sandy would pop his head in to see our progress. "You coming to help or just supervising?" I asked. Marvin and I work well together. He was cutting off the ends of this towel holder, and I told him he was just creating work for himself. "Oh, snap," he said.

"Teamwork makes the dream work," I said.

It came out really beautiful, and Mom loved it in her Mom way.

"That's very nice," she said. "I don't want you doing too much for just me." My other mission was for me to get her all-new furniture for her living room, but she shot that down. "Angie, don't waste that money." Her concession was to let me order her a new mattress. She's not like me. When I get something new, I want everything new, honey. A new house while I'm at it!

After all that work, Marvin and I were ready for the reward of good cooking. I looked at Sug helping Mom, and I reflected on our mother, so independent for so many years, feeling vulnerable in this new chapter of her life. Thanks to her and Sug, the table was set with beautiful food, like stuffed flounder and collard greens with ham hocks. And of course, there was the rice I had to eat so much of as a kid in order to stretch the budget. We all sat at the table and joined hands.

"Mom, do you mind if I say grace?"

"Of course, Angie."

"Lord, thank You for the food before us, the family beside us, and the love between us. You have given us so many blessings, and we have worked to honor Your gifts. We are grateful You let us be in this moment together. Thank you. In Jesus's name we pray."

I pulled Sug's and Marvin's hands closer to me and gave each a kiss on the backs of their hands. I looked at Mom across the table, all of us sitting once more in the house she provided us.

"Mom," I said, "I'm really proud of you. Everything we've got is because you worked so hard."

"You said you would make me proud, Angie," she said. "And you have. You've made me the proudest mother at Breeding Tabernacle."

That moment lives in my heart. I keep it because there will be a time she will not be here, and I have to accept that as much as I accept any of my own new chapters. As we grow, we have to make way for Generation Next. Amazing people like my little nephew Myles,

Marvin's son with the megawatt smile. Or his middle son, Chris, a.k.a. Private First Class Fox. I am so proud that he has followed in the military footsteps of his army dad and chose to become a Marine. And I look at Sug's daughter, Sharday, a gorgeous replica of my sweet sister. I see such promise in these children and young adults, and it is a joy and honor to pass on to them the lessons that I have learned in life.

I am still Angie from Indianapolis, Indiana, and I am still trying to make my mom proud. I have told you to keep thinking of new goals, and it's only fair that I share mine. The new note to put in my Bible.

I want to be an advocate for women, and anyone who gets counted out. As a businesswoman, I would like my hair line to go more international and continue to reach a more diverse base of customers. I want to produce more and more projects that provide opportunities for artists to make *their* dreams come true. I want to grow as an actress, and I think working opposite Denzel Washington or Samuel L. Jackson would challenge me to a great performance. Sam Jackson and I did *Kill Bill* together, but his part was small. In fact, he wrote it himself. "There ain't gonna be six fine women in a movie with Quentin Tarantino and I don't have a part," he told me.

When he was on the set, I point-blank asked him how in the world he had time to do so many films.

"Viv, it's because I do the work," he said. "I'm an actor. Everybody's so worried about being a star and being famous, and I do the work. And so do you."

I'm so blessed to be doing the work. I am proud that my films have grossed over $2 billion worldwide. I just finished playing the President of the United States in a science fiction film called *Crossbreed*. I was talking to a reporter about it, and she asked if I realized I was making history.

"For doing a sci-fi movie?"

"No," she said. "You're the first African American woman to play the president in a film."

The director, Brandon Slagle, told *The Hollywood Reporter* I was chosen because they needed "someone who could light up a room but also has a commanding presence," a.k.a. the Head Chick in Charge. I'm finally getting the roles I've wanted to play.

I used to make resolutions. Now I plant seeds. I could never have predicted what job was going to lead to another. I believe me being politically involved and getting out there and standing up for my beliefs led to me playing the President of the United States. Now I plant seeds by doing independent films with young talent and young directors, who later can reward me with bigger and better roles. They will remember that I showed up and supported them. If I believe in the work and in the vision of the director, I take a pay cut and I get them exposure. And I plant that seed.

As I worked on this book, I realized that I wasn't just sewing these seeds for me. I think about the women I came up with: Halle, Angela, Latifah, Jada. And the women who planted the seeds to make our dreams possible: Diahann Carroll, Ruby Dee, Lena Horne. But the breakthrough for me was to see that now we have these leading ladies breaking through as producers: Viola Davis, Kerry Washington, Gabrielle Union, Regina King—all incredibly talented women who are making things possible. Head Chicks in Charge. We always knew we had it in us. They used to tell us, "African American women in leading roles won't get ratings. A black woman can't lead a movie, and black people don't sell overseas." Really? Because people across the waters seem to want to see how we dress, how we dance, how we sing . . .

I stuck to it, just like I want you to stick to it. I am so excited to hear about all the wonderful things you are going to do. Please keep me posted on your progress and consider me a friend and a cheer-leader.

I want to leave you with the promise I give to all the people I care about. **I'm blessed to be your favorite sister girl. I may go far, but I will never leave you.**

Hugs and kisses,

Vivica A. Fox

THESE ARE A FEW OF MY FAVORITE THINGS (AND BEAUTY SECRETS!)

1. Downy fabric softener. You're gonna laugh, but I just love the smell. When I travel, I fill up a spray bottle with Downy, and I mist it on the bed and linens in my hotel room. It just reminds me of home.

2. Wolford underwear. I am a G-string type of girl, and Wolford is my go-to. They fit like a second skin, with edges that never show, so I can wear them on the red carpet. Bonus: They're nice and light, and you don't feel like you're gonna get a damn yeast infection from them.

3. Christian Louboutin and Jimmy Choo shoes. They simply make the best shoes. I just bought a pair of little booties the

other day. They are like artwork, and they make for fabulous conversation pieces.

4. Noxzema cleansing cloths. I take it old-school! I always use them to take off my makeup.

5. La Perla lingerie. Expensive but freaking beautiful. I mean, the lace, the detail . . . everything. It lies on your body like butter. I like bright colors, because I like a hint of color underneath a suit or a blouse.

6. Dermalogica skin-care products. I swear by them. I also keep the Dermalogica antioxidant hydramist toner spray with me when I travel. If I am on a long flight and feeling a little dehydrated, I spray that right on.

7. Jo Malone candles. I wear the Jo Malone Red Roses fragrance, so of course I love the Red Roses candles. But I have fallen in love with the Pine & Eucalyptus blend. It's only available around the holidays, so I stock up. It makes my home smell like a spa. People walk in and they say, "Damn, and your house smells good, too!"

8. Spanx. Go to the original for shapewear, and give thanks to the creator, Sara Blakely. There's a reason she is a billionaire! I have no problem with a good old undergarment.

9. My airplane blankie. You won't see me using one of them blankets on the plane. I bring my own, one that I know is nice and clean! And yes, I spray a little of that Downy fabric softener so it smells good.

10. Wine. Don't let people tell you that you have to spend a lot. Francis Ford Coppola's Pinot Noir is an inexpensive red that you can count on. For white, try Kendall-Jackson's Chardonnay. Now, champagne is worth the splurge. Personally, I love Cristal. And if you're making me a martini, I like a *dirty* martini. That's when you add just a touch of the brine from the olive jar. I love it with olives stuffed with blue cheese.

11. My go-to floral arrangement. I always send two dozen multicolored roses arranged in a vase. It's nice and colorful, and it smells delicious. And I stay true to the design because I want people to just see them and say, "Vivica is thinking of me." This past Mother's Day, my mother told me that when they were coming to the door, she said, "I know my baby bought me this." It's nice to have a signature that speaks before the card.

12. Sneakers. I wasn't into sneakers until a few years ago when my knees were like, "We need a break." I think there's something chic about Adidas sneakers, white or black, that go as well with a warm-up suit as a leather jacket. I have also fallen in love with Tory Burch sneakers for when I travel. They're so cute, and they feel a little high-end for the lower price point.

13. Jewelry. I am such a diamond girl, and Candy Ice is my favorite jewelry designer. I love the rose-cut diamond slice floral ring. When I went through a breakup, I bought myself a ball-and-chain diamond bracelet. And when I broke up with my husband, I bought myself three beautiful watches, one by Harry Winston and two by Chopard.

14. CORE Hydration water. It's my newest discovery. It keeps you hydrated and matches your body's pH balance. I just know I like it.

15. P.F. Chang's and California Pizza Kitchen. These are two of the chains I favor. And by "favor," I mean that I know the menus by heart. At P.F. Chang's, I love the Hong Kong sea bass, and the lobster-and-shrimp fried rice. At CPK you'll see me getting a salad or, if it's a cheat day, a pizza-and-pasta combo.

What's In My Bag at All Times

My girlfriends make fun of me because my bag is so heavy that it's like I'm carrying around a drugstore. Here are the essentials:

- First, the bag itself: Christian Louboutin makes a beautiful one that just goes perfectly with my Louboutin shoes. I like Louis Vuitton because it is such a staple—everyone knows what you have when you walk into a room with their bag. And, of course, Céline. I treated myself to a Céline black luggage tote last year. It is simply the ultimate bag for the professional woman.

- I have to have clear mascara because my brows have got to be in place. My favorite mascara is Maybelline Great Lash clear mascara.

- I always have my little Brookstone fan for what I call my private summers. Hot flash? Chill out.

- Honey, whether it's a headache or standing all day on set, I want to be ready with Aleve. It's also a great anti-inflammatory. When you're standing in heels all day, your knees get so swollen.

- Jao Refresher hand sanitizer. I meet a lot of people and I can't afford to get sick, so I always have a two-ounce bottle with me. It has a light moisturizer built in, so it doesn't dry my hands.

- It's nice to have a few Burt's Bees Lip Shimmers in different colors. They have about fourteen shades from light Champagne to dark Plum, so believe it or not, I have a whole bunch of different ones in my bag. My favorite is Peony. They have just a little pop of peppermint, so you're just ready to kiss!

- My lip gloss is Sisley Phyto-Lip Star in White Diamond.

- My go-to eyeliner is by Stila. I use the Stay All Day Waterproof one in a charcoal shade.

- If you are as much of a brow girl as me, you want the Brow Wiz pencil from Anastasia Beverly Hills. It's a fine-point retractable pencil that lets you draw in little hairs or define the line, and then you turn it around and use the brush to blend the color. But that's not enough for me. I always have an additional brow brush. Always.

- My powders are the MAC C7 and C4 Studio Fix Powder Plus foundations. They are not heavy, but they do the job.

- Pens and highlighters. I keep them handy so I can mark up scripts. I highlight my lines, and also things that I think could be punched up or worked on.

My Own Top Five Favorite Performances

1. *Independence Day*

   It's a sentimental favorite of mine because it was such a breakout for me. I especially love my running scene, when the aliens first start hitting all the targets. I give an amazing hair toss. I save the kid, and then the dog—and later, the First Lady! At the premiere they clapped for me during the scene, and I had such a Sally Field moment of "You like me!"

2. *Soul Food*

   My favorite scene is when I am walking on Lakefront Trail in Chicago with my on-screen son Brandon Hammond, who was about twelve at the time. He tries to get something by me and I say, "I carried you for nine months, went through twenty-three hours, forty-five minutes, and ten seconds of labor. Wiped your little butt while your lil' ding-a-ling pee-peed in my face. So Mama knows when you're up to something." People come up and say that to me, and I finish the line with them.

3. *Kill Bill*

   Love it, love it. Of course the scene for me is when Uma and I fight and trash the house in Pasadena. Quentin Tarantino had a special booty light trained right on my butt to make sure people could see it. The movie is a classic, so I know a hundred years from now film students will be looking at my booty and it will hold up!

4. *Set It Off*

   So many good scenes in that film, but the best for me is right after the robbery. A lot of people do my monologue on social media as an acting exercise or to just be dramatic. They always tag me and I love it.

5. *Two Can Play That Game*
   I won't spoil nothing, but there is a scene in a bar where Morris Chestnut says my character's name, Shanté. I have to turn, and it is just such a movie-star moment. It gets me every time.

Fox Film School: Eleven Astonishing Performances to Learn From

1. Pam Grier in *Jackie Brown*
   You know she is my all-time idol, but her performance in this Quentin Tarantino film goes beyond just my love of her. Throughout the movie, you see Pam thinking as Jackie, right from the start. The whole movie centers on her planning this heist, so it makes sense. So often you see her working out a plan and solving a problem without even saying a word. Also it was good to see an older woman being sexy and strong. I would love to do that with Quentin as well. *Hint, hint.*

2. Faye Dunaway in *Mommie Dearest*
   Whatever you think of the movie, Faye acted her ass off. She is ferocious and scary and sometimes winning, even as she is always mean. Yes, the wire-hanger scene is my favorite, because it is so freaking scary. It's been parodied so much, but if you watch it, I guarantee you your heart will be in your throat and you'll be as frightened as Christina. She is going to reach through that screen and hit *you*. The sad thing is that Faye so inhabited the role, invited Joan Crawford in so fully, that I think she got stuck being

Joan. You gotta learn when to let a character go. But if I am going through the channels, Faye stops me every time.

3. Denzel Washington in *Training Day*
Directed by the amazing Antoine Fuqua. Denzel is just so sexy. That charisma jumps off the screen, and it's so important because you have to believe that this is a dirty cop you wouldn't mind gettin' dirty with.

4. Meryl Streep in *The Devil Wears Prada*
She could have just been a bitch, right? But instead she is such a charming bitch. I love that scene where she dresses down Anne Hathaway's character for acting like she is above caring about fashion. She goes into all the details of how many people are involved in any craft, how one decision leads to another, choices that influence other artists and create jobs and industries. Artists should cheer when they see that scene because she could be talking about any of our projects. And watch how she moves! She is having this one-sided conversation, and she is always just keeping her hands busy so the monologue is active and engaging. It's just brilliant.

5. Will Smith and Jaden Smith in *The Pursuit of Happyness*
I was traveling during the premiere, so I saw it late.
A friend warned me, "Better bring that Kleenex."
He was right. No spoilers, but the scene where Will's character, Chris, goes to hug his son in the day care after all they have been through together—homelessness but never hopelessness . . . Okay, now I'm crying again.

6. Viola Davis in *Fences*

   She blew me away as Rose. How do you do a performance on Broadway 114 times, then bring it to the screen, and still bring the urgent spirit of that monologue? She just breaks open after her husband tells her he is having a baby with another woman. You believe every word, and you believe that Rose is fighting to find the strength to hold on to her family. Then, when she takes in that baby and delivers that line to Denzel, oh my God: "From right now . . . this child got a mother. But you a womanless man." By the time she says that, you are right there with her.

7. Debra Winger and Shirley MacLaine in *Terms of Endearment*

   I can't pick one because the chemistry makes their performances so entwined. They make you believe that these two women have real history as mother and daughter. How often do we see that realness on-screen?

8. Diana Ross in *Mahogany*

   I think I was eleven when it came out, and we saw it right away. "There goes my girl," I said. "That's my woman right there." Diana is just so glamorous in the film, and she gives it her everything. When she loses it and lets fame go to her head, it is so real. "They love me! Mahogany!"

9. Richard Roundtree in *Shaft*

   Here is this black detective, practically a superhero, whose very presence demands respect. It's astounding that this was his first feature film, but I think it's telling that he was a model beforehand. He knows just how to hold himself for the camera, and he fills the screen.

10. Charlize Theron in *Monster*

I love her presence, and I admire that she showed her versatility right out of the gate. So smart for a pretty girl to play a nasty-looking serial killer. People talk about the thirty pounds Charlize put on and the fake teeth, but it's all her in that role. She portrays the conflict of fear and rage within Aileen Wuornos.

11. Louis Gossett Jr. in *An Officer and a Gentleman*

Marine Gunnery Sergeant Emil Foley! He dominates *every* scene. You know that the script originally called for a white man to break Richard Gere down so he could build him back up. Louis took it and made it his. He brings such decency to Foley. Even when he just seems *so* mean, you know it's to make Richard's character a better man.

A Playlist to Amp Up Your Hustle

Whether it's for a workout or a date night, you will be ready!

1. "Rock with You"—Michael Jackson
2. "Lucky Star"—Madonna
3. "We Will Rock You"—Queen
4. "Formation"—Beyoncé
5. "Sweet Child o' Mine"—Guns N' Roses
6. "I Wanna Be Your Lover"—Prince
7. "Don't Stop Believin' "—Journey
8. "Roar"—Katy Perry
9. "Remember the Time"—Michael Jackson
10. "If I Could Turn Back Time"—Cher
11. "No Matter What They Say"—Lil' Kim
12. "Never"—Heart
13. "Run the World (Girls)"—Beyoncé

14. "Upside Down"—Diana Ross
15. "1999"—Prince
16. "Better Be Good to Me"—Tina Turner
17. "Livin' on a Prayer"—Bon Jovi
18. "Real Love"—Mary J. Blige
19. "Everywhere"—Fleetwood Mac
20. "Walk This Way"—Aerosmith and Run DMC
21. "We Are the Champions"—Queen

The Playlist for When You're Alone in Your Castle

Tupac and Kenny G? Why not? I don't know what it is about "Songbird," but it makes me feel like I'm on a boat in Jamaica.

1. "One of Those Days"—Whitney Houston
2. "Everything She Wants"—Wham!
3. "Muscles"—Diana Ross
4. "All Eyez on Me"—Tupac Shakur
5. "Careless Whisper"—George Michael
6. "Songbird"—Kenny G
7. "The Lady in My Life"—Michael Jackson
8. "No Ordinary Love"—Sade
9. "My Heart Will Go On"—Celine Dion
10. "I Will Always Love You"—Whitney Houston

ACKNOWLEDGMENTS

When I was a young woman in search of my dream in New York City, I would often walk by the Flatiron Building on Fifth Avenue. Its wedge shape always stuck out to me, and I was that Indy girl looking up at this beautiful, unique tower. When I went to my first meeting at St. Martin's Press, I walked into that same building I loved all those years ago. As soon as I met the wonderful people there, I felt the next chapter of my life—becoming an author—happening with them. They respected me as a talent, valuing my own story as a grown woman in my fifties, and supporting me in my dream of creating other stories to share. With so many writers I respect calling St. Martin's Press home, I knew it was the right place for me to be.

I am so grateful to my editor, Elizabeth Beier. I love your energy and commitment to excellence. And also your honesty. You inspired me to, as you told me, hit a homer right out of the park while wearing Christian Louboutins. Thanks also to my St. Martin's family, including Jennifer Enderlin and Sally Richardson, Meg Drislane, Cathy Turiano, Mike Storrings, Karen Masnica, John Karle, Brant Janeway, Jonathan Bennett, Beatrice Jason, and Nicole Williams.

To my literary agent, Albert Lee: You have so much soul, and you maintain a passion for making good books. You are so thorough, writing the most detailed emails I have ever received. Each one is a mini-book, but an enjoyable read.

I so value my friendship with my publicist, BJ Coleman. You made my dream come true by connecting the dots to make me an author. We share so many passions, from fashion to branding, and I am grateful that are always making sure that I slay the game.

I say that Kevin Carr O'Leary is part of my rainbow coalition. For the first months, when we spoke only on the phone, I thought you were black. Imagine my surprise when I finally met you in person. You are my new white chocolate brother, and I thank you for capturing my voice and my journey so perfectly. I loved working with you.

To my business partner, Lita Richardson: You are such a gem, and I thank you so much for your wisdom and guidance. I am indebted to you for always reminding me about the *business* in show business. The day I met you, my pretty lawyer, was one of the biggest blessings of my life.

I thank every single person who supported me in my career as I went from Indianapolis to Hollywood. Special thanks to my mother, Everylena Fox, and my siblings, Alecia "Sugie" Williams, Marvin "Brotha Marv" Fox, and William "Sandy" Fox. To all of my extended family and friends: I love you guys and you all know *exactly* who you are.

To my fabulous fans: I know without you, there would be no me.

And I thank God for my beautiful journey. No matter what is given to me or taken from me, I find strength in knowing that I will always be a blessed child of God.

INDEX